Authentic Christianity

Authentic Christianity

A Fresh Grip on Life

RAY C. STEDMAN

MULTNOMAH PRESS
PORTLAND, OREGON 97266

Cover design by Phil Malyon and Judy Quinn
Photograph by Tom Ballard/EKM-Nepenthe

AUTHENTIC CHRISTIANITY
© 1975 by Ray C. Stedman
Published by Multnomah Press
Portland, Oregon 97266

Printed in the United States of America

Library of Congress Cataloging in Publication Data

Stedman, Ray C.
    Authentic Christianity.

    Reprint. Originally published: Waco, Tex. : Word Books, 1975.
    1. Christian life—1960-   I. Title.
BV4501.2.S738   1984   248.4   84-20536
ISBN 0-88070-072-6 (pbk.)

84 85 86 87 88 89 90 – 10 9 8 7 6 5 4 3 2 1

CONTENTS

To Elaine
loyal helper, loving critic,
a woman to be proud of.

PREFACE

This is the book I have wanted to write above all others. It deals with the very heart of the gospel, the most important truth contained in the pages of Scripture. That truth is the new covenant of which the Lord Jesus spoke when he passed the cup at the Last Supper and said, "This is the blood of the new covenant which is shed for many for the forgiveness of sins."

To understand the full implications of that new covenant is to discover the most liberating secret in the word of God. It is, as Paul put it, "Christ in you, the hope of glory." Upon that fundamental union with Christ all God's plans for present victory over evil and future manifestations of glory squarely rest.

It is my hope and prayer that God will use this book to open the eyes of many to this central truth and lead them to experience, in this present life, the glorious liberty of the sons of God!

Ray C. Stedman

1
THE GREAT IMITATION

The Christian life begins with an encounter with Jesus Christ. It cannot be otherwise. "He who has the Son has life; he who has not the Son of God has not life" (1 John 5:12).

Many things may lead to that encounter and much of it may be intensely religious, but until a person responds to the promise of Christ and receives him as Lord there is no possibility of eternal life. That "receiving" may be so effortless and gentle as scarcely to be chronicled, as with a child; or it may be spectacular and dramatic, like the Apostle Paul; or peaceful and with little or no feeling except warmth, like John Wesley's conversion; or even tortuous and painful, as with St. Augustine. However it occurs, it must occur before there can be any hope of living a Christian life.

The Bible Says . . .

That encounter with Christ, so vital to becoming a Christian, assumes a number of things which rest upon the written record of the Bible. Consequently, some knowledge of the Bible and/or of its teachings is essential to believing in or receiving Christ. It is the biblical account of the crucifixion and resurrection of Jesus which gives us any reason for believing that Jesus is alive and available to us; that Jesus can, by the Holy Spirit, actually come to live within a human being and so entwine his own life with that person that from then on the two must be regarded as essentially one. It is the biblical account of the life and character of Jesus that gives us any basis for assuming that Jesus is truly the Savior he claimed to be and that he has the power and wisdom to deliver and free all who come to him. You recall that Jesus said, "Come to me all who labor and are heavy laden, and I will give you rest" (Matthew 11:28); and "I am the light of the world; he who follows me will not walk in darkness, but will have the light of life" (John 8:12).

No Other Way

But no matter how clearly one may understand *who* Jesus is and *what* he can do, and even *how* he does it (by the principle represented in his cross and resurrection, or what some like to call "the plan of salvation"), nevertheless, until the human will responds to the invitation of Jesus and chooses to receive him, obey him, and follow him there can be no impartation of eternal life. All offers of salvation in the New Testament are directed to the will to make the choice of surrendering to the Lordship of Jesus. One does not become a Christian by intellectually comprehending the historical facts about Jesus. By the same token one does not become a Christian by grasping the theological implications of his death and resurrection. One does not become a Christian by adhering to certain moral and ethical standards which Jesus taught. Nor does one become a Christian by seeking to relate one's life to God apart from Jesus Christ. Rather, one becomes a Christian by asking Jesus to come in as Lord and by then believing that he is capable of doing it and has actually done it by means of the Holy Spirit. Whenever (and however) that occurs, what is essentially a miracle takes place, though it may well be without outward demonstration or feeling. A new quality of life (called eternal life) is imparted to that individual and he is "made alive in Christ." It is this divine action that makes him a Christian, and nothing else. "He that has the Son has life; he that does not have the Son does not have life." It is that simple.

Signs of Life

But that is just the beginning. As a human baby, fresh from its mother's womb is truly a person, though its life may be undeveloped, so a newly regenerated individual is truly a Christian and shares the life of Jesus. This is true even though there is much to be learned and experienced before that life achieves anything that can properly be called maturity. Happily, however, certain manifestations of the new life do appear soon. Perhaps the easiest to recognize is a sense of peace and well-being, especially in terms of one's feelings about God. It is, as Paul tells us, the result of God's Spirit bearing witness with our human spirit that we are now the children of God. And that sense of peace is made more intense and lasting as we come to realize the full implications of sins forgiven through our relationship to Christ. This release from guilt is a large part of the peace Christians experience.

Another element soon present in the new Christian is a sense of belonging to a family. We learn that we are not alone, but have become members of a large and ever-growing family. As members of that family, we have many brothers and sisters to relate to and enjoy while at the same time we have continual access to our heavenly Father through prayer and love. For many the most joyful part of that new life is release from the fear of death and what lies beyond. To have the certain hope of heaven rather than the fear of hell is a relief beyond all expressing.

Because of these elements present in varying degrees at varying times, many new Christians experience intense excitement and joy. The Bible becomes a fresh and exciting book, and meeting with other Christians is a continual joy. The change in their own attitudes and outlook is apparent to everyone, and they find it difficult to understand why they did not become Christians years earlier.

Three Possible Choices

This initial state of euphoria may continue for weeks or even months. But inevitably, sooner or later, the old natural life begins to reassert itself. The glow begins to fade from Christian worship, and Bible reading becomes less and less rewarding. Christian fellowship in meetings and individual contact becomes dull and routine—old habits of thought and action reassert themselves. This is a critical time when one of three possibilities may occur. First, the young Christian continues his decline to the point of dropping out of all Christian relationships, neglects his Bible totally, has little or no time for prayer, loses interest in spiritual matters entirely, and is finally living no differently than he was before he became a Christian. It is true there may be occasional periods of remission with the possibility of eventually establishing a fairly consistent Christian life, but in the majority of cases there is no return, at least for many years, and grave doubt is raised as to whether the individual ever became a Christian at all.

The second possibility is that he becomes aware of his cold and rebellious heart, is frightened by the thought of regressing to what he was before, and casts himself in repentance and frustration upon the Lord anew, renewing his trust in God's promises, and perhaps seeking the help of older, more experienced Christians and thereby returning to a state of peace and joy. This cycle may be repeated many times until it becomes the pattern of his experience and he comes to think of it as normal Christianity. On the other hand he may, happily, learn something from each repeated cycle till eventually his eyes are opened to the truth that will deliver him from his roller-coaster experience and he becomes a settled, stable, Spirit-led Christian.

The third and most likely possibility is that the new Christian may discover what millions of others before him have learned: It is possible to avoid the pain and humiliation of repentance and renewal by maintaining an outward facade of spiritual commitment, moral impeccability, and orthodox behavior. In so doing he can preserve a reputation for spiritual growth and maturity that is satisfying to the ego and seems to gain much in the way of opportunities for service and the commendation of the Christian community. Such a Christian life-style is usually so prevalent and so little condemned that the new

Christian can hardly be blamed for adopting it and regarding it as the expected thing. He drifts into it with scarcely a pang, little realizing that it is a total fraud, a shabby imitation of the real thing. He would be deeply offended if anyone should call him a hypocrite. To him hypocrisy is a deliberate attempt to deceive others, and his own commitment to the doctrine, moral standards, and practice of Christianity is deep and sincere. But in reality he is a hypocrite because the peace he claims to have is present only while his circumstances are untroubled, the joy he sings about seldom shows on his face, and the love he is forever extolling is reserved only for those who please him. It is all a giant sham, though for the most part an unconscious one. He may be a true Christian in whose heart Christ dwells, but except for rare moments (usually of desperation or high ecstasy) he does not live the Christian life. The quality of life may be moral, often even generous, and it certainly is religious, but it is anything but Christian. Actually it is virtually the same life he lived before receiving Christ, but now it is covered by a thin Christian glaze, a veneer which quickly disappears when events become irritating, difficult, or distressing.

Different More Than Somewhat

This may seem like a harsh judgment to many. True Christianity in certain circles is equated with doctrinal purity, and whenever true teaching is adhered to it is very difficult for those who view life this way to accept the charge that they are not yet living an authentic Christian life. But it must be remembered that true Christianity is more than teaching—it is a LIFE. "He who has the Son has life"!—remember? That life is more than mere morality, it is more than doctrinal accuracy, it is more than inoffensive gentility. It is positive, not merely negative; it is radical, not superficial; it is humble, not self-praising; it is compassionate, not indifferent; it is courageous, not retiring. It is a far cry indeed from the mild compatibility that passes for Christianity in thousands of churches across the land. The Great Imitation is so widely accepted as genuine Christianity that the real thing is often regarded as a threat or a heresy whenever it appears.

It is the purpose of this book to trace the sharp distinctions between the phony and the genuine. We shall be guided wholly by the revelation of Scripture, for the Word of God is the only sufficient guide to distinguish truth from error. We shall explore together a major passage from Paul's second letter to the Corinthians—chapters 2:14 to 6:13. In this passage Paul helps the Corinthians to distinguish between authentic Christianity, as he himself lived it, and the pale imitation that many of them had mistaken for the real thing. Then the apostle takes them on, step by step (and us with them) into an understanding of the enormous enrichment that awaits those who learn to live by the New Covenant, which gives life, and not by the Old, which kills. The treatment of the passage will not be theological (in the bad sense of that term), nor will it be devotional (horrible word), but intensely practical and forthright. If you are interested at all in radical and authentic Christianity, read on.

2
THE REAL
THING

It has always seemed unfair to me that many churches (and some individual Christians) keep careful records on how many converts they make to Christianity, but never keep any records at all on how many they drive away from Christ. Fairness would seem to dictate that both sides of the ledger should be maintained. For the fact is, churches often turn far more people from Christ than they ever win to him, and frequently it is the most zealous and orthodox of Christians who are doing the driving away. The reason is, as we have seen, that though they may indeed be true Christians themselves, the life they are manifesting is false Christianity. It is as phony as a three-dollar bill.

False Out of True

True, there is a false Christianity which is practiced by those who aren't Christians at all. There are many religious frauds who have never been real Christians, and there are apostates who give every appearance of being Christian for awhile and then throw the whole thing over. But surely the most subtle stratagem ever devised by the Tempter to deceive and delude men is to take genuine Christians who truly know Jesus as the living Lord and Savior and mislead them into practicing a sham Christianity which they sincerely believe is the real thing. It can't, of course, be detected by a doctrinal statement or adherence to a creed, for this type of phony Christianity is always orthodox. It is frequently very zealous and feeds upon consecration services and dedication meetings. It uses all the right terms and behaves in the proper, orthodox manner, but the net result is to drive people from Christ rather than bring them to him.

In sharp contrast to this, there is the real thing—authentic Christianity as it was intended to be. When it is manifested, it never requires advertisement or publicity. It has a fascination about it that will draw people like flies to honey. True, it may antagonize many when they find out what its secret is, but the initial character of authentic Christianity is to attract and compel admiration. That was certainly its effect in the life of Jesus of Nazareth. There is, of course, no clearer demonstration possible of what real Christianity looks like than was evident in the life of Jesus. This was Christian life in its purest and most utterly consistent form.

An Apostle's Example

But the trouble with that demonstration, for many people, is that they feel Jesus had an edge over the rest of us in that while he was undoubtedly man, he was also God, and from that Divine heritage he drew strength to resist evil that the rest of us do not have. That is a highly debatable point, but we shall not enter into the argument here. Rather, let's turn to one of the many other passages of Scripture which describe authentic Christianity in terms of someone we may feel a bit closer to—at least at first. Since authentic or radical Christianity is the end result toward which all the Scriptures move, there are many passages in both the Old and New Testaments which could be used to guide us to this discovery. But we shall choose one particular selection from Paul's second letter to the Christians at Corinth. This letter is one of the most biographical of all Paul's letters. In it the apostle gives us insight into his own experiences and reveals to us in the clearest terms the secret of his great ministry.

The first one and one-half chapters of Second Corinthians indicate that Paul was being challenged by certain Christians at Corinth. They had been affected by some Jewish Christians from Jerusalem who suggested that Paul was not a genuine apostle at all because he was not one of the original twelve, and because he taught certain things that went beyond the law of Moses. Claiming that he was not a real apostle, they insisted his brand of Christianity was not real Christianity. One of the Devil's favorite tricks is to brand the truth as a big lie, and that was what was going on at Corinth.

Five Unmistakable Marks

Paul's response to this is to describe for us the nature of his ministry. It has, as we shall see, five marks or qualities which cannot be successfully imitated. These qualities are always present whenever real Christianity is being practiced, and no matter how clearly false Christianity may try to copy them, it can't be done. They are inimitable. They have nothing to do with personality or temperament and therefore are attainable by anyone who discovers their secret. And they are not limited to one period of time, but are just as genuine when manifested in the twentieth century as in the first.

We shall begin our journey of discovery at the fourteenth verse of the second chapter of Second Corinthians. In this one verse are hidden three of the marks of genuine Christianity, and the remaining two are found in the verses that follow. "But thanks be to God, who in Christ always leads us in triumph, and through us spreads the fragrance of the knowledge of him everywhere" (2 Corinthians 2:14).

Unquenchable Optimism

The first of the five marks is found in the very first phrase, "thanks be to God." One unmistakable mark of radical Christianity is that it is a thankful life even in the midst of trial and difficulty. It is a kind of *unquenchable optimism*. You can see it clearly in the Book of Acts where a note of triumph runs right through from beginning to end despite the dangers, hardships, persecutions, pressures, and perils that the early Christians experienced. The same continual note of thanksgiving is reflected in all of Paul's letters as well as those of John, Peter, and James.

The kind of thanksgiving referred to throughout is genuine. It is really and truly felt. There is nothing put on or artificial about it. It is a far cry from the phony imitation that is sometimes seen in Christians today. Some people think they are required to repeat pious and thankful words even though they don't really believe them just because the Scriptures say that is the way Christians should act. Many have settled for a form of Christian stoicism, a grin-and-bear-it attitude which even a non-Christian can adopt when there's nothing much he can do about a situation. But that is a long way from Christian thankfulness. To listen to some sermons today one would think that Christians are expected to screw on a smile and go around saying, "Hallelujah, I've got cancer!"

But authentic Christianity does not do that. It feels all the hurt and pain of adverse circumstances as much as anyone else, and does not enjoy them in the least degree. But it does see an end result being produced (not only in heaven, someday, but right now, on earth) that is so desirable and glorious it is worth all the pain and heartache. Therefore, it can do nothing else but rejoice. An authentic Christian is confident that the same Lord who permitted the pain to come will use it to bring about a highly desirable end, and can, therefore, be genuinely thankful even in the midst of perplexity and sorrow.

There is an outstanding example of this in Acts 16 when Paul and Silas found themselves at midnight thrust into an inner dungeon in the city jail of Philippi. Their backs were raw and bloody from the terrible flogging they had received at the hands of the Roman authorities, and their feet were fastened immovably in stocks. The future ahead was very uncertain; they didn't know what might happen to them in the morning. There was no one around to be impressed by a show of courage and no one to whom they could look for intervention or help. Yet despite such a discouraging outlook, Paul and Silas saw something about the situation that made them literally break into song.

No one could accuse them of being phony or of putting up a good front in an effort to keep up their spirits. They were genuinely thankful to God and began to praise him at midnight because they knew that despite the apparent rebuff and lack of success, their objective had been accomplished. The church they longed to plant in Philippi now *could not be stopped.* That made them break out in praise and thanksgiving. Of course, they knew nothing at that moment about the earthquake that would jar their chains loose and set them free. They had no premonition at all of being set free, but were simply manifesting the inevitable mark of having found *the radical secret of Christianity*—unquenchable optimism and thanksgiving.

Unvarying Success

The second mark is closely linked to the first and is found in the next phrase, "who in Christ always leads us in triumph." Note how Paul puts it, "he *always* leads us in triumph." Not occasionally, or sometimes, but always. The apostle makes perfectly clear that the Christianity which he has experienced presents a pattern of *unvarying success.* It never involves failure but invariably achieves its goals. It involves, as we have seen, struggle and hardships and tears, but though the struggle may be desperate, it is never serious. It issues at last in the accomplishment of the objectives sought. Even the opposition encountered is made to serve the purposes of victory.

We must remember that these high-sounding words are not mere evangelical pep talk. They were not uttered by a pastor to a well-dressed congregation in a twentieth-century church to give them a vicarious thrill as they momentarily felt the challenge of faith. Instead, they were written by a man who bore on his body the brand-marks of Jesus and who had endured much difficulty, endless disappointments, and bitter persecution with great pain. Yet he could write with rugged truthfulness: "He always leads us in triumph."

This certainly did not mean that Paul's plans and goals were always realized, for they were not. He wanted to do many things that he was never able to accomplish. In the ninth chapter of Romans Paul tells us how he hungered to be used as a minister to Israel—"my kinsmen according to the flesh." He even expressed the willingness to be cut off from Christ if only the Israelites would be delivered. But he never achieved that objective. It is not his plans that are in view here, but God's. The triumph is Christ's, not Paul's. But the invariable mark of authentic Christianity is that when any individual has learned to discover its radical secret there is never a failure. God cannot be thwarted in his will. Every obstacle becomes an opportunity and success is inevitable.

The Liberty of Prison

It is this principle of invariable triumph which Paul describes in the first chapter of his letter to his friends at Philippi. He is now a prisoner in the city of Rome, confined to a private, rented home but chained day and night to a member of Caesar's Imperial Guard. Things look bad for him. He must soon appear before Nero Caesar to answer Jewish charges that could mean his life. He can't travel about the empire, preaching "the inexhaustible riches of Christ." And he cannot even visit the churches he founded. What a time for discouragement. Yet no letter of the New Testament reflects more confidence and rejoicing than that of Philippians. The reason for this confidence, Paul says, is twofold. He writes, "I want you to know, brethren, that what has happened to me has really served to advance the gospel" (Philippians 1:12). Then he lists two evidences to prove his point.

First, he says, ". . . it has become known throughout the whole praetorian guard, and to all the rest that my imprisonment is for Christ" (Philippians 1:13). The praetorian guard is the Imperial bodyguard. Since he is a prisoner of Caesar's, he must be guarded by Caesar's picked guard. The guard was made up for the most part of sons of noble families who were commissioned to spend a few years in Nero's palace guard. Later on the group would become the kingmakers of the empire and were responsible for the choice of several succeeding emperors. They were impressive young men—the cream of the empire.

Anyone who can read between the lines a bit will see what is happening here. It is clear that the Lord Jesus, in his role of King of the earth, has appointed Nero to be the chairman of the Committee for the Evangelization of the Roman Empire. Nero doesn't know this, but then emperors seldom know what is really going on in their empires. Remember that when the time came for the Son of God to be born in Bethlehem, his mother and her new husband were 70 miles away, living in Nazareth. So God commissioned Emperor Augustus with the task of getting Joseph and Mary down from Nazareth to Bethlehem. Augustus felt strangely moved to issue an Imperial Edict that everyone should go to his hometown to be taxed, and that did the trick! So in this case Nero has given orders that his Imperial Bodyguard should have charge of the Apostle Paul. And every six hours one of the splendid young men was brought in and for six hours chained to the Apostle Paul!

I suggest that if you want to feel sorry for anyone that you feel sorry for this young man. Here he is, trying to live a quiet, pagan life and every so often he is ordered out and chained to this disturbing man who says the most amazing things about one called Jesus of Nazareth, risen from the dead. As a result, one by one these young men were being won to Christ. It is what you might call a chain reaction! If you doubt that this is what was taking place, then look at the next to the last verse of the Philippian letter. There Paul says, "All the saints greet you, especially those of Caesar's household" (Philippians 4:22). Here is a band of young men, the political center of the empire, who are being infiltrated and conquered for Christ by an old man in chains who is awaiting trial for his life. It is not at all unlikely that some of the young men who accompanied Paul on his later journeys came from this very band.

This incident is a magnificent revelation of the strategy of God and, incidentally, of the weakness of human planning by contrast. No human mind could have conceived this unique approach to the very heart of the empire. We humans are forever planning strategies for fulfilling the Great Commission, but what we come up with is usually banal, routine, unimaginative, and relatively ineffective. The noteworthy thing about God's strategy is that it often takes the form of active opposition.

Progress by Opposition

That is what is recorded in the early chapters of Acts. The church in Jerusalem was growing by leaps and bounds. Some 2,000 to 5,000 Christians were gathering together weekly and enjoying the tremendous fellowship and excitement. Yet it was all contained within the city walls. When God wanted to spread these good things among the nations, he permitted sharp opposition to arise. As a result, the early Christians were driven throughout the empire, all except the apostles.

Since having learned to glimpse God's hand in these acts of opposition, I have begun to read missionary reports in a different light. Of late years there have been many reports in missionary magazines saying in one way or another, "Terrible things are happening to our country. The doors are closing to the gospel; opposition is arising, the government is trying to suppress all Christian witness, and we missionaries must soon pack up and get out." Now there is no question but what missionaries need much concerted prayer, and the national Christians are in terrible and immediate danger. Nevertheless, when I read such reports, I have learned to say, "Thank God. At last the missionaries are being forced to relinquish control of the churches and the national church is taking over." In Ethiopia, before World War II, the missionaries were driven out for twenty years, but when they came back in they found that the gospel had spread like wildfire, and there were far more Christians than if the missionaries had been allowed to stay. China is a similar story.

Bolder Brothers

Paul makes a second point in his letter to the Philippians to support his claim that the things which happened to him had only served to advance the gospel. He says ". . . most of the brethren have been made confident in the Lord *because of my imprison-*

ment, and are much more bold to speak the word of God without fear" (Philippians 1:14). Because Paul was a prisoner, the Roman Christians were witnessing far more freely throughout the city than they would have done otherwise. It was at this time that the first official Roman persecution against the Christians was beginning. Many, therefore, were afraid to speak of their faith. But when they saw that God was in complete charge of matters—not Nero, nor the Jews—they were emboldened to proclaim the gospel. As a result, there was far more effective outreach going on in Rome than even if Paul had been free to preach at will. This fact has always suggested to me that perhaps the best way to evangelize a community would be to start by locking all the preachers up in jail! Other Christians might then begin to realize that they, too, have gifts for ministry and begin to exercise them in effective ways. Sometime I would like to try it.

Living Letters

As we who live in the twentieth century look back upon this first-century incident, we can see still a third proof of Paul's claim that even he himself could not see at the time. If we had been with Paul in that hired house in Rome and had asked him, "Paul, what do you think has been the greatest work you have been able to accomplish in your ministry, through the power of Christ?" what do you think he would have said? I feel sure his answer would have been: "the planting of churches in various cities." It was to these churches that his letters were written, and it was for them that he prayed daily. He called them, "my joy and crown" and spent himself without restraint for them.

But now, looking back across these twenty

intervening centuries we can see that the planting of
these churches was not his greatest work after all.
Every one of the churches he planted has ceased its
testimony long ago. In most cases, the very cities in
which they existed lie in ruins today. But the work of
Paul which has persisted to this day and has had permanent and increasing value throughout the centuries has been the letters that he wrote when he was
locked up and could do nothing else! Those letters
have changed the world. They are among the most
powerful documents ever known to men. No wonder
Paul could write, "Thanks be to God, who in Christ
always leads us in triumph." It is an unmistakable
mark of authentic Christianity.

Unforgettable Impact

The third unmistakable mark follows immediately. ". . . through us [God] spreads the fragrance of the knowledge of him [Christ] everywhere." Here is another of the beautiful symbols by
which God teaches truth. It is that of fragrance, of
perfume. Paul clearly implies that the Christian life,
lived as it ought to be, is a fragrance, not only to men
but to God. He enlarges further on this thought: "For
we are the aroma of Christ to God among those who
are being saved and among those who are perishing,
to one a fragrance from death to death, to the other a
fragrance from life to life" (2 Corinthians 2:15-16).

Most men have had the experience of being in a
room when a strikingly beautiful woman enters. Before she came in she had applied a touch here and
there of Chanel #5, and as she passes through the
room, she leaves behind a lingering.fragrance. All the
males in the room take note of it, consciously or unconsciously. Perhaps weeks or months later they may
smell the fragrance again and immediately the image

of that beautiful woman flashes into their minds. The fragrance has made her unforgettable.

That is the picture Paul gives here. There is something about authentic Christianity when it is encountered that leaves an *unforgettable impression*. The Christian who has discovered this secret makes an enduring impact; he is never taken for granted by anyone. As Paul suggests, the impact may be in one of two directions. He either increases opposition to Christ (death to death) or he leads toward faith and life (life to life). If your life is one that reflects radical, authentic Christianity, then you are making people either bitter or better by contact with you. But one thing cannot happen: people will never remain the same. Those who are determined to die are pushed on toward death by coming into contact with authentic Christianity. Those who are seeking to live are helped on into life. Jesus certainly had this quality about him. No one ever came into contact with him and went away the same.

Many commentators on this passage have felt that Paul had in mind here a typical Roman triumph. When a Roman general returned to the capital after a successful campaign, he was granted a triumph by the senate. A great procession passed through the streets of Rome displaying the captives which were taken in the course of the conquest. Some went before the chariot of the conqueror bearing garlands of flowers and pots of fragrant incense. They were the prisoners who were destined to live and return to their captured country to govern it under Roman rule. Other prisoners followed behind the chariot dragging chains and heavy manacles. These were doomed to execution, for the Romans felt they could not trust them. As the procession went on through the cheering crowds, the incense pots and fragrant flowers were to the first group "a fragrance from life unto life" while the same aroma was to the second group "a fragrance of death to death."

This is the effect of the gospel as it touches the world through the person of a Christian. If it is authentic Christianity that is in view, it will be a fragrance to God of Jesus Christ, no matter what, but to men it is either of death to death or of life to life. Of course, if it is phony Christianity that is manifest, it will simply be a bad smell! I once saw a card that said, "Old fishermen never die—they only smell that way." That surely describes false Christianity. It never dies; it only smells that way.

Unimpeachable Integrity

The fourth mark of genuine Christianity is found in verse 17 of chapter 2: "For we are not, like so many, peddlers of God's word; but as men of sincerity, as commissioned by God, in the sight of God we speak in Christ."

Remember, that is not a description of Christian pastors but simply of Christians. It has great application to pastors and others in the ministry, but its primary reference is to common, ordinary Christians who have learned the secret of radical Christianity. They can be described in two ways, negatively and positively. Negatively, they are not peddlers. The word means a huckster, a street salesman. Occasionally I hear Christian witnessing described as "selling the gospel." I cringe when I hear that because I don't believe Christians are meant to be salesmen for God. The idea here is that of a street hawker who has certain wares which he feels are attractive and which he peddles on the corner as people are passing by. He makes his living by peddling his wares.

Much Christian preaching and witnessing can be described that way. Men pick out certain elements from the Scriptures which have a power to attract people, and they major on these themes. Healing is a case in point. It is a legitimate subject for study and practice, but when singled out and harped on continually, especially when large offerings are connected with it, healing can quickly lead to hucksterism. Prophecy can serve the same purpose. If a man is known only as a prophetic teacher, I am troubled about him, for he has picked out something that is attractive from the Word, and if that is all he ever teaches, he is not declaring the whole counsel of God. He is a peddler, making a living by hawking certain wares from the Scriptures.

Four Qualities—One Mark

Paul says authentic Christianity is not like that. It is characterized by four things. First, we are "men of sincerity." In other words, we are to be honest men. We must mean what we say. Sincerity marks the highest demand of the world upon men. The world admires sincerity and feels it is the acme of character, but here it is but the beginning, the minimum expectation from a Christian. The least one can expect from a true Christian is that he himself believes what he says and seeks constantly to practice it.

Next, Paul says we are "commissioned by God." Here is the idea of purpose. We are not to be idle dreamers or wasters with no definite objective in view. We have been commissioned as military officers are commissioned, given a definite task and specific assignments—so the Christian is commissioned. We are purposeful people with an end in view, an object to attain, a goal to accomplish, and we do not merely preach or witness as though that were a goal in itself. We are sent to accomplish something by our witnessing.

The third factor is that we do all this "in the sight of God." This indicates an attitude of openness to investigation, of transparency. To walk in the sight of men permits many deviations and contradictions behind the facade, but to walk in the sight of God is honest transparency. This does not mean sinlessness, but rather that there can be no hiding of sin when it occurs. It is to know that there are no hidden areas to God, that we are being evaluated and tested by the purity and knowledge and wisdom of God. A man who walks in the sight of God isn't interested in putting up a good front. He is perfectly trustworthy. You can trust his golf score. And if you get young people to do this, they can be trusted even in the back seat of a car.

The last characterization is that "we speak in Christ." What quality does that indicate? Authority! Paul says it clearly in chapter 5, "We are ambassadors for Christ, God making his appeal through us" (vs. 20). Ambassadors are authorized spokesmen. They have power to act, to bind. Thus authentic Christians are not powerless servants. We speak words and deliver messages which heaven honors.

All this adds up to *unimpeachable integrity*. Men of sincerity, purpose, transparency, and authority are utterly trustworthy. They have integrity. You can ring a gold coin on their conscience. Their word is their bond, and they can be counted on to come through. They are responsible and faithful individuals. That is the fourth great mark of real Christianity.

At this point in the text of the Bible there comes a chapter division. This is unfortunate for it serves to divide two things which belong together. The apostle has not finished his line of argument. It is best to ignore the division and read right on, to find the fifth mark of authentic Christianity: "Are we beginning to commend ourselves again? Or do we need, as some do, letters of recommendation to you, or from you?" (2 Corinthians 3:1).

Undeniable Reality

It is apparent that the apostle is aware that he is beginning to sound highly complimentary to himself. He knows there are some in Corinth who will immediately take these words in that way. Indeed, it is obvious from his words that some had even suggested in previous correspondence that the next time he came to Corinth he bring letters of recommendation from some of the Twelve in Jerusalem! They were thinking of Paul as though he were a man entirely like themselves: so continually praising himself that no one would believe him until he had confirmation from more objective sources. But Paul says to them:

You yourselves are our letter of recommendation, written on your hearts, to be known and read by all men; and you show that you are a letter from Christ delivered by us, written not with ink but with the Spirit of the living God, not on tablets of stone but on tablets of human hearts (2 Corinthians 3:2-3).

He is saying, in effect, "You want letters of recommendation to prove that I am an authoritative messenger of God? Why, you yourselves are all the recommendation I need. Look what has happened to you. Are you any different? Have there been any changes in you since you came to Christ through my word? Your own hearts will bear witness to yourselves and before the world that the message which you heard from us and which has changed your lives is from God." In 1 Corinthians 6 Paul made reference to "the immoral, the idolators, the adulterers, the homosexuals, the thieves, the greedy, and the drunkards" which he had found in Corinth. "Such," he said, "were some of you." But now they had been washed, sanctified, and justified by the name of the Lord Jesus Christ. These changes were proof of reality. The Corinthians had written to Paul about the joy they now had and the hope and meaning which had been brought into their lives. They described to him the deliverance from shame and guilt they had experienced, the freedom from fear and hostility, from darkness and death, which was theirs. So he says, "This is your confirmation. You yourselves are walking letters from God, known and read by all men, written by the Spirit of God in your hearts."

Here is the last mark of genuine Christianity. It is that of *undeniable reality,* a change which cannot be explained on any other terms than God at work. Paul did not need letters of recommendation when this kind of change was evident in the lives of his hearers. Once I heard of a Christian who had been an alcoholic for years and then was converted. Someone asked him, "Now that you are a Christian, do you believe the miracles of the New Testament?" He answered, "Yes, I do." The other man said, "Do you believe that story about Jesus changing water into wine?" He said, "I sure do." The other said, "How can you believe such nonsense?" The Christian replied, "I'll tell you how; because in our house Jesus changed whiskey into furniture!" That is the mark of authenticity. Such a marked change cannot occur except under the impulse of a powerful relationship that substitutes the love of Christ for the love of drink.

There are the five unmistakable signs of genuine Christianity: unquenchable optimism, unvarying success, unforgettable impact, unimpeachable integrity, and undeniable reality. They are always present whenever the real thing is being manifested. Mere religion tries to imitate these marks, but is never quite able to pull it off. By comparison with these marks, phony Christianity is always shown up to be what it is—a shabby, shoddy imitation that quickly folds when the real pressure is on. The remarkable thing is not that men seek to imitate these genuine graces, for we have all been hypocrites of one kind or another since our birth. The truly remarkable thing is that becoming a Christian does not of itself guarantee that these Christian graces will be manifest in us. It is not *being* a Christian that produces these, but *living* as a Christian. There is a knowledge we must have and a choice we must make before these virtues will be consistently present. It is the knowledge of this secret which the Apostle Paul goes on to give us. We shall examine it in careful detail in chapter three.

3
THE SECRET

In the midst of the five marks of authentic Christianity which came into focus as we read Paul's description of his own experience and ministry, there was a question which I deliberately passed by. It is found in 2 Corinthians 2:16: "Who is sufficient for these things?" Take that question seriously. Try to answer it! Who is, indeed, sufficient for things like these? Who can find in himself the sufficiency to manifest consistently a cheerful, confident spirit . . . an ability always to come out on top . . . a powerful influence on others . . . a complete trustworthiness . . . and such a realistic demonstration of these qualities that no one is ever in doubt about them? What

course can we take that will teach us how to live like
this? What book can we read that will have this effect? What fantastic discovery of the hidden powers
of the human spirit will produce a life like this? Who
is sufficient for these things? The question hangs in
the air, waiting for an answer.

Siren Voices

Immediately a half dozen or so possibilities rush
into mind, for the question is so important that half
the world's activity is devoted to finding an answer.
Flip through the pages of any current magazine and
almost any product advertised subtly or blatantly
suggests that it is the fulfillment of your search.
"Drink Dipse-Cola, and really live!" "Do your friends
ignore you? Try Charm deodorant, the underarm se-
curity!" "Read 'How To Be A Phenomenon,' the
amazing new success story." "Sign up for our six-
week course, 'The Power Ploy,' it will change your
life!" "Find the romance you've always wanted, sail
on the *S. S. Slopover* to the Islands of Mystery." What
a cacophony of voices—hammering out the message
that they offer what we are looking for. "Try it; you'll
like it!" But by the time you're twenty-five you know
they're all a lie.

Paul does not leave us groping for an answer to his
searching question. In 2 Corinthians 3:4-6 he gives
us his forthright answer:

> *Such is the confidence that we have through Christ
> toward God. Not that we are sufficient of ourselves
> to claim anything as coming from us; our suffi-
> ciency is from God, who has qualified us to be
> ministers of a new covenant, not in a written code
> but in the Spirit; for the written code kills, but the
> Spirit gives life.*

He puts the great secret before us in unmistakable terms: "Our sufficiency is from God!" Lest anyone miss the implications of that, he puts the same truth negatively: "Not that we are sufficient of ourselves to claim anything as coming from us." Nothing coming from us; everything coming from God! That is the secret of human sufficiency.

Live It—Don't Waste It

To live from such a base, says Paul, is to be "a qualified minister of a new covenant." He contrasts this sharply with the old covenant—the "written code which kills." To live with nothing coming from us and everything coming from God is to live in the Spirit, who is continually giving Life, with a capital L. It is this secret which produced the confident spirit that characterized Paul and made him spread the fragrance of the knowledge of Christ everywhere he went. The language he used reminds us immediately of the words of Jesus to his disciples: "Apart from me, you can do nothing" (John 15:5). Neither Jesus nor Paul means to imply that there is no human activity possible without reliance upon God. Both the world and the church are full of examples to the contrary. But what Jesus and Paul both teach is that activity which depends upon human resources for its success will, in the end, accomplish nothing. It will have no permanent value. Men may praise it and emulate it, but God will count it for what it is—wasted effort. Just such a life is described in the plaintive question of T. S. Eliot.

> *All our knowledge brings us nearer to our ignorance,*
> *All our ignorance brings us nearer to death,*
> *But nearness to death no nearer to God.*
> *Where is the life we have lost in living?*
> *(from "The Rock")*

Where, indeed? Candor forces us to admit that we deliberately waste a good deal of our life in useless dreaming and profitless activity. But not all of it! There are times when we give it the old college try, times when we are earnest and serious and do our very level best to act as we ought and do what we should. The results often appear very impressive to us, and even to others, but when we think of our approaching death, it all seems rather vain and futile. It is then we ask, "Where is the life we have lost in living?"

The Basis of Life

The apostle indicates that the secret of an effective, meaningful life lies in what he terms "the new covenant." This "new covenant" is that to which Jesus refers when he passed the cup to his disciples at the institution of the Lord's Supper. "This is my blood of the new covenant which is poured out for many for the forgiveness of sins." This cup, taken with the bread, is to remind us of the central truth of our lives: Jesus died *for* us in order that he may live *in* us. It is his life in us that is the power by which we live a true Christian life. That is the new covenant.

It is important to understand the meaning of the word *covenant*. There are, according to Paul, two covenants at work in human life. One is the new, which he describes as "nothing coming from me, everything from God." The other is the old, which is in direct contrast to the new and can therefore be described as everything coming from me and nothing coming from God.

The root idea of covenant, both in Paul's day and ours, is that of an agreement which forms the basis upon which all further relationship rests. If two men go into business together, they form a partnership. The terms of their relationship are carefully spelled out so they will have a framework within which to work. Marriage is also a type of covenant in which a man and a woman agree together to share all they have and to stick together against all obstacles till death. Nations sign treaties with one another to determine the conditions under which they will work together. All these examples are forms of covenants, and it is apparent from these that a covenant is fundamental and essential to all human endeavor. But the most fundamental covenant of all is that which forms the basis of human life itself. We may not often think of it in this way, but no activity is possible to us that does not rest upon an underlying covenant. We could not talk, sing, walk, speak, pray, run, think, or breathe without that covenant. It is fundamentally an arrangement made by God with man whereby man is furnished the life and energy he needs to perform what God wants him to do. Man does not provide his own energy. He is a dependent creature, needing a constant supply from God the Creator in order to live or breathe.

Now the great thing that Paul declares to us in this passage and which is confirmed by many Scriptures, both in the Old and the New Testaments, is that this fundamental arrangement for living comes to us in one of two ways. There is an "old" way which, as we shall see in the next chapter, is linked inextricably with the Mosaic law, "The written code which kills." But through Jesus Christ there is a "new" way which gives life that is unquenchably optimistic, characterized by unfeigned success, makes unforgettable impact, consists of unimpeachable integrity, and confronts the world with a testimony of undeniable reality. It is through having discovered the implications of this new covenant that the apostle finds himself qualified to live as God intended him to live, and it is through discovering these same implications for ourselves that we shall find ourselves qualified by God to live as God intends us to live today.

How Paul Found the Secret

Since the apostle uses his own experience as the example of the kind of life he has in view, it will be helpful to trace the way and the time that he came to learn this transforming truth for himself. If you think it all came to him in that one dramatic moment in the dust of the Damascus road when he discovered the true identity of Jesus Christ and yielded himself to his lordly claims, then you are far from the truth. It is true that Paul was born again at that moment; it is true that he understood for the first time that Jesus was indeed the Son of God; it is true that the center of this ardent young Pharisee's life was forever changed from living for his own advancement to desiring the eternal glory of Jesus Christ. But it may be of great encouragement to many of us who struggle in the Christian life to learn that Paul also went through a period of probably ten years after his conversion before he began to live in the fullness of the new covenant. And it was during this time that, from God's point of view, he was an abject failure in living the Christian life!

Two Declarations in Damascus

If we pick up Luke's account of Paul's conversion from the ninth chapter of Acts, we can piece together from several other Scriptures the full account of what happened to produce the tremendous change in his life. Here is a description of what happened after the experience of the Damascus road:

> *For several days he was with the disciples at Damascus. And in the synagogues immediately he*

> *proclaimed Jesus, saying, "He is the Son of God."*
> *And all who heard him were amazed, and said,*
> *"Is not this the man who made havoc in Jerusalem*
> *of those who called on this name? And he has come*
> *here for this purpose, to bring them bound before the*
> *chief priests" (Acts 9:19b-21).*

It is clearly apparent from these words that it all happened within a very few days after Paul's conversion and his baptism at the hands of Ananias. Paul began immediately, with characteristic vigor, to *proclaim* (herald, announce) the deity of Jesus ("He is the Son of God"). This truth he had learned in the glory of the light that flamed about him on the road to Damascus. Then Luke, without giving any indication in the text whatever, goes on in his account to something which did not take place for at least several months after the above events and which may not have occurred for as long as three years afterward: "But Saul increased all the more in strength, and confounded the Jews who lived in Damascus by proving that Jesus was the Christ" (Acts 9:22).

Note that Paul's (or Saul's) message is here said to be in the form of "proving" that Jesus is the Christ. There is a great difference between *proclaiming* Jesus as the Son of God and *proving* that he is the Christ. Luke only hints at what made the difference in his phrase, "Saul increased all the more in strength," but Paul himself tells us in more detail what happened in his letter to the Galatians.

From Proclaiming to Proving

Many scholars consider the Galatian letter to be the earliest of Paul's epistles. Whether it is or not is uncertain, but it is clear that in it Paul defends his apostleship and describes what happened to him after his conversion. He writes:

> *But when he who had set me apart before I was*
> *born, and had called me through his grace, was*
> *pleased to reveal his Son to me, in order that I*
> *might preach him among the Gentiles, I did not*
> *confer with flesh and blood, nor did I go up to*
> *Jerusalem to those who were apostles before me, but*
> *I went away into Arabia; and again I returned to*
> *Damascus (Galatians 1:15-17).*

We learn from this account that what served to greatly strengthen young Saul at this time was that he went away into Arabia and then returned to Damascus. What did he do in Arabia? There is no Scripture that tells us, but I do not think it is difficult to know. We need only imagine the shock to this young man's life which his conversion produced to realize that he desperately needed time to go back through the Old Testament Scriptures and find how his discovery of the truth about Jesus of Nazareth related to the revelation of the prophets which he had trusted ever since he was a child. As a Pharisee and based on what he knew of the Scriptures, he was convinced that Jesus of Nazareth was a fraud. Now he knew better, yet somehow, somewhere, he must work out the mental confusion this new discovery produced in him. Arabia supplied the opportunity.

Into Arabia he went, the scrolls of the Old Testament tucked under his arm. As we might well surmise, he found Jesus on every page. How the old, familiar passages must have glowed with new light as beginning with Moses and all the prophets the Spirit of God interpreted to him the things that belonged to Jesus. It was no wonder that when he returned to Damascus he came "greatly strengthened." And no wonder, too, that armed with his new-found knowledge, Paul went into the same synagogues where he first "proclaimed" that Jesus was the Son of God, and there, turning from passage to passage, "proved" (Greek: "to knit together") that Jesus was the Christ (the Messiah).

A Basket Case

But now things took a turn for the worse. To young Saul's chagrin the Jews of Damascus were not at all responsive to his powerful arguments. Luke tells us what happened:

> *When many days had passed, the Jews plotted to kill him, but their plot became known to Saul. They were watching the gates day and night, to kill him; but his disciples took him by night and let him down over the wall, lowering him in a basket (Acts 9:23-25).*

What a burning humiliation to this dedicated young Christian! How confused and puzzled he must have been as all his dreams of conquest in the name of Jesus were brought to this sudden and degrading halt. It was humiliating to be let down over the wall in a basket like a common criminal escaping from the reach of the law! How shameful, how discouraging! He stated later that it was both the lowest point in his life and the beginning of the greatest discovery he ever made. But now he slips off into the darkness of the night, bewildered, humiliated, and thoroughly discouraged.

The Same Old Story

Where does he go from there? Luke tells us immediately, "And when he had come to Jerusalem he attempted to join the disciples; and they were all afraid of him, for they did not believe that he was a disciple" (Acts 9:26).

Paul's own account agrees with this exactly. In Galatians 1:18-19 he says, "Then after three years I went up to Jerusalem to visit Cephas [Peter] and remained with him fifteen days. But I saw none of the other apostles except James the Lord's brother." How he managed to break through the fear barrier to see these two men is given us by Luke:

> *But Barnabas took him, and brought him to the apostles {Peter and James, the Lord's brother}, and declared to them how on the road he had seen the Lord, who spoke to him, and how at Damascus he had preached boldly in the name of Jesus. So he went in and out among them at Jerusalem, preaching boldly in the name of the Lord. And he spoke and disputed against the Hellenists; but they were seeking to kill him (Acts 9:27-29).*

It is a familiar pattern. Once again the ardent young Christian is determined to persuade the Greek-speaking Jews (Hellenists) that Jesus is the promised Messiah of the Old Testament. Once again a plot against his life is set in motion. It is the Damascus story all over again.

Get Out!

But at this point there occurs another of those gaps in Luke's account which we must fill in from Paul's own account elsewhere. Luke does not tell us what young Saul's reaction is to the opposition he received to his message from the Jerusalem Jews. But knowing his ambitious and dedicated heart, it must have been one of severe discouragement. At any rate, years later, in his great defense to the Jerusalem mob when he was arrested in the temple precincts and was saved from certain death only by the timely intervention of the Romans, he mentioned this occasion. In Acts 22 he tells us,

> *When I had returned to Jerusalem and was pray-*
> *ing in the temple, I fell into a trance and saw him*
> *saying to me, "Make haste and get quickly out of*
> *Jerusalem, because they will not accept your tes-*
> *timony about me" (Acts 22:17-18).*

It is surely understandable that young Saul would seek the comfort of the temple at this discouraging moment. Again his efforts to bear a convincing witness for Christ had failed, once again men were seeking to find an opportunity to kill him, and he had no positive results with which to encourage himself. No wonder he went into the temple to pray. And there, to his discouraged disciple, the Lord Jesus himself appeared. But his message was anything but encouraging. "Get out of Jerusalem," said Jesus, "they will not receive your testimony concerning me." At this point Saul began to argue with the Lord:

> *And I said, "Lord, they themselves know that in*
> *every synagogue I imprisoned and beat those who*
> *believed in thee. And when the blood of Stephen thy*
> *witness was shed, I also was standing by and ap-*
> *proving, and keeping the garments of those who*
> *killed him" (Acts 22:19-20).*

In these words Saul gave himself away. We can now see what he was depending upon for success in his efforts at witnessing. It is apparent that he saw himself as the one eminently qualified to reach the Jews for Christ. His argument says in effect, "Lord, you don't understand this situation. If you send me out of Jerusalem you are going to miss the opportunity of a lifetime. If there is anyone who understands how these Jews think and reason, it is I. I was one of them. I speak their language. I know how they react. If anyone has the qualifications to make them listen, it is I. I do not come to them as one unacquainted with their background. I too am an Israelite, a Hebrew of the Hebrews, circumcised on the eighth day, of the tribe of Benjamin. I was a Pharisee like they are. I walked before the law blameless. I even persecuted the church, as they are now doing. Why, when the martyr Stephen was killed, it was I who kept the garments of those who murdered him. Lord, don't send me away. I have what it takes to reach these men. Don't miss this opportunity."

Jesus' answer is abrupt and to the point. Paul tells us himself, "And he said to me, 'Depart; for I will send you far away to the Gentiles'" (Acts 22:21). What a shattering blow! How crushed young Saul must have been! But to indicate how the church agreed with the Lord at this point, Luke tells us, "And when the brethren knew it [the plot to kill Saul], they brought him down to Caesarea, and sent him off to Tarsus" (Acts 9:30).

"Go Home Young Man"

Tarsus was Paul's hometown. There is no tougher place to go as a Christian than back home. Paul had tried his best to serve his new-found Lord with all the ability and energy he could muster. But it amounted to exactly nothing. In fact, at this point, Luke records a rather astonishing thing after Paul's exile to Tarsus:

> *So the church throughout all Judea and Galilee and Samaria had peace and was built up; and walking in the fear of the Lord and in the comfort of the Holy Spirit it was multiplied (Acts 9:31).*

When the consecrated blunderer was gone, the church had peace. When the dedicated disputer was eliminated, the church began to grow! Is that not amazing? Saul goes off to Tarsus to nurse his wounds, his ego shattered and his hopes lost in despair. For ten years he is not heard of again, not until an awakening breaks out in Antioch of Syria and the church in Jerusalem sends Barnabas down to investigate. When Barnabas found that "a large company was added to the Lord" (Acts 11:24), he knew help was needed. "So Barnabas went to Tarsus to look for Saul; and when he had found him, he brought him to Antioch." It was a different Saul who came to Antioch with Barnabas. Chastened, humbled, taught of the Spirit, he began to teach the Word of God, and from there launched into the great missionary thrust that would take him eventually to the limits of the Roman Empire and spread the gospel with explosive force throughout the world.

What made the difference? Writing to the Corinthians many years later Paul makes one brief reference to the event that triggered a line of teaching that would culminate in a clear understanding and acceptance of what he came to call "the new covenant." The Corinthian church had written to Paul and brazenly suggested to him that he would be more effective if he would boast once in awhile in his accomplishments. To this the apostle replied in his second letter, chapter 11: "If I must boast, I will boast of the things that show my weakness. The God and Father of the Lord Jesus, he who is blessed for ever, knows that I do not lie" (2 Corinthians 11:30-31).

What he is going to say will be such a shock to them that he takes a solemn vow that he is telling them the truth, otherwise they may think he is joking or playing with them. Then he tells them what his boast is: "At Damascus, the governor under King Aretas guarded the city of Damascus in order to seize me, but I was let down in a basket through a window in the wall, and escaped his hands" (2 Corinthians 11:32-33).

"That," says Paul, "is my boast. That is the greatest event of my life since my conversion. When I became a basket case, then I began to learn the truth that has changed my life and explains my power." What was that life-changing truth? Let Paul put it in his own words, from his letter to the Philippians.

> *If any other man thinks he has reason for confidence in the flesh, I have more: circumcised on the eighth day, of the people of Israel, of the tribe of Benjamin, a Hebrew born of Hebrews; as to the law a Pharisee, as to zeal a persecutor of the church, as to righteousness under the law blameless. But whatever gain I had, I counted as loss for the sake of Christ. Indeed I count everything as loss because of the surpassing worth of knowing Christ Jesus my Lord. For his sake I have suffered the loss of all things, and count them as refuse, in order that I may gain Christ (Philippians 3:4b-8).*

The word he uses for "count them as refuse" refers to common, barnyard dung. What he once regarded as qualifying him to be a success before God and men (his ancestry, his orthodoxy, his morality, and his activity) he now regards as so much manure compared to depending upon the working of Jesus Christ within him. He has learned how to shift from the old covenant (everything coming from me, nothing coming from God) to the new covenant (nothing coming from me, everything coming from God), which gives life. He is no longer highly qualified to be utterly useless but is able to say: "Our sufficiency is from God, who has qualified us to be ministers of a new covenant."

Have you become a basket case yet? Have you reached that place which Jesus described as "blessed"? "Blessed are the poor in spirit, for theirs is the kingdom of heaven." To be "poor in spirit" is to be utterly bankrupt before some demand of life, and then discover it to be a blessing because it forced you to depend wholly upon the Lord at work in you. That is where you learn the truth of the new covenant, and nowhere else. We have much to learn yet about *why* it works, but you can only find out *how* it works when you discover it in your own experience.

4
TWO SPLENDORS

God loves visual aids. He has scattered them all
over the earth and hung them in the sky. Jesus made
rich use of God's visuals to help in understanding
spiritual truth. "Consider the lilies of the field, how
they grow"; "It is harder for a camel to go through the
eye of a needle than for a rich man to enter the kingdom of God"; "Cast not your pearls before swine, lest
they turn and rend you"; "You are the salt of the
earth," etc. It seems highly likely that the whole
world of nature was created to illustrate, on the level
of the physical and visible, what is going on all the
time in the invisible, spiritual realm. Elizabeth Bar-
rett Browning put it exactly,

Earth's crammed with heaven;
And every common bush aflame with God.
But only those who see take off their shoes,
The rest sit round it—and pluck blackberries!
                                        ("Aurora Leigh," bk VII)

Two Faces of Glory

To help the Corinthians (and us) understand what he meant by "the old covenant" and "the new covenant" the Apostle Paul used two very helpful visual aids. They are borrowed from the story of the giving of the law from Mt. Sinai and the subsequent conduct of Moses with the people of Israel. He first calls attention to the glory of Moses' face:

> *Now if the dispensation of death, carved in letters on stone, came with such splendor that the Israelites could not look at Moses' face because of its brightness, fading as this was, will not the dispensation of the Spirit be attended with greater splendor? (2 Corinthians 3:7-8).*

The old covenant, which he calls "a dispensation of death," was aptly symbolized by the shining of Moses' face when he came down from the mountain with the law "carved in letters on stone." There was a certain glory or splendor about the law. It attracted people and awakened their admiration and interest. That's what glory always does; it is captivating and attractive. To this day the law retains that attractiveness. All over the world the Ten Commandments are held in high regard, even by those who regularly break them (which includes us all). Men pay lip service to them as the ideal of life, even though they may say they are impractical and impossible to keep. Everywhere men dream of achieving a dedication which will enable them to fulfill these glorious ideals.

But the point Paul seeks to make is that in the new covenant there is an even greater splendor. It is far more attractive and exciting than the law. As we have just seen, any reliance on the old covenant after one has experienced life in the new is like going back to dung and manure! And just as the glory of the old covenant has its symbol (the shining face of Moses), so the new covenant has its symbol as well. It is given by the apostle a little further on in the passage and is obviously intended to be set in contrast with the face of Moses. He says, "For it is the God who said, 'Let light shine out of darkness,' who has shone in our hearts to give the light of the knowledge of the glory of God *in the face of Christ*" (2 Corinthians 4:6).

There are the two splendors—the face of Moses and the face of Jesus Christ. Both are exciting, but one much more than the other. They stand for the two covenants, or arrangements, by which human life is lived. Both have power to attract men, but one is a fading glory and the other is not. The unredeemed world lives continually by looking at the face of Moses. The Christian can live by either, but never both at the same time. It is always one *or* the other at any given moment of a Christian's life. "No man can serve two masters," said Jesus, "either he will hate the one and love the other, or he will be devoted to the one and despise the other." So in the true Christian's life, the activity of each moment derives its value from whether he is, at that moment, symbolically looking at the face of Moses or at the face of Jesus Christ.

The Trouble with Law

At this point we must seek to understand more clearly something of great importance. Someone may well raise the question, "Why does Paul link the old covenant with the law and call it a "dispensation of death" when in Romans 7 he says that the law is "holy, just and good"? How could the shining face of Moses which came as a result of spending forty days alone with God be a symbol of something which kills? As a matter of fact, Paul himself raises the same question in his discussion of the law in Romans 7 when he says, "What then shall we say? That the law is sin?" (Romans 7:7). His sturdy response is, "By no means!" And after showing that it was by means of the law that he found out the extent of his sin, he adds, "So the law is holy, and the commandment is holy and just and good."

It is in Romans 8:3 that the apostle gives us the clue which explains this enigma: "For God has done what the law, *weakened by the flesh,* could not do." The problem, therefore, is not the law; it is what the law must work with, that is, the flesh. The word "flesh" does not refer here to the meat and bones that make up the body, but is an equivalent term for fallen human nature—human nature acting apart from Christ. The law was given, in any of its forms, only and solely because the flesh exists. There is no need for law if there is no flesh. Paul said to Timothy,

> . . . *the law is not laid down for the just but for the lawless and disobedient, for the ungodly and sinners, for the unholy and profane, for murderers of fathers and murderers of mothers, for manslayers, immoral persons, sodomites, kidnapers, liars, perjurers, and whatever else is contrary to sound doctrine* (1 Timothy 1:8-10).

Civil War Within

These verses shouldn't be read as though Paul were referring only to pagans, heathens, criminals, and perverts. Christians, even the best and saintliest of them, are sometimes "lawless and disobedient," are "unholy" or even "profane," all too frequently "liars," "perjurers," and many "Christian" sins are caught up in the phrase, "Whatever else is contrary to sound doctrine." Certainly the "flesh" is at work in Christians, and whenever it is, the law is required. The law is made for the flesh. It has no reason for existence apart from it. The flesh requires the law, for "by the law is the knowledge of sin."

Since this is so clearly true, it helps us to see that the essential conflict between the old covenant (the face of Moses) and the new covenant (the face of Jesus Christ) is, in reality, the struggle between the flesh and the Spirit. To the Galatians Paul wrote: "For the desires of the flesh are against the Spirit, and the desires of the Spirit are against the flesh; for these are opposed to each other to prevent you from doing what you would" (Galatians 5:17). It is because of this inevitable tie between the flesh and the law that Paul, in 2 Corinthians, refers to the law as a "ministration (or dispensation) of death" and says that the "written code kills." In reality, it is the flesh which produces death and which kills, but the law, though it be holy, just, and good cannot be separated from it.

The preceding arguments may seem a bit ponderous, but I urge you to think them through carefully, for perhaps nothing has contributed more to the present weakness of the church than a failure to understand the nature and character of the flesh. It may greatly help us to see this clearly if we go back to the beginning and learn how the flesh came into existence and what its essence is.

Man Without Flesh

When Adam came from the hand of God, he was a perfect man, as God intended man to be. He was, therefore, acting by the power of God. Everything he did was accomplished by the indwelling Spirit of power. We know this from the analogy to Jesus who was the Second Adam. Jesus tells us repeatedly that whatever he did or said was not done out of any energy or might of his own, but as he plainly put it, "the Father who dwells in me, does his works" (John 14:10). He was living by the new covenant, "everything coming from God, nothing coming from me." In fact, he said, "The Son by himself can do nothing" (John 5:19). It was thus that Adam lived, before the Fall. When he tended the garden, he did so by the energy and power of God. When he named the animals, he named them by the wisdom and power of God. Adam brought to each task the fullness of Divine resources, available to whatever degree was required by the task itself. This is, of course, what man was and is intended to be, the bearer and dwelling place of God. Adam was the "house" of God, and all that he did was a manifestation of the power of God. The choice of activity was left up to Adam. That was his part. He was the chooser; God himself was the doer. Adam could do anything he wanted, go any place within the garden he chose, eat anything he liked—except one thing. Put beyond his *right* to choose but not beyond his *power* to do so, was one tree—the tree of the knowledge of good and evil.

The Great Removal

One day, in connivance with his wife, Adam made that fatal choice. The instant he did so, the "new" covenant ceased to be active in his life, and the "old" covenant came into existence. Of course, the new was not properly called "new" then, for at the time it was the only arrangement for living that Adam knew.

And, of course, the old covenant was not "old" to him, but something brand new which he experienced only after he had chosen to disobey God. The terms "new" and "old" have meaning only in relation to us, not to Adam, but I use them this way to show that they were the same in his experience as they are in ours.

Since everyone who has ever lived since Adam was made in the image of fallen Adam, we can understand something of what happened when Adam ate the forbidden fruit. The Spirit of God was immediately removed from his human spirit. His spirit retained a memory of the relationship it once enjoyed, but it was left darkened and restless, filled with both guilt and fear, and unable to contact the God it knew existed. This is why Adam and Eve immediately hid themselves. They realized they had no defense against attack and were naked. It is into this same condition that every human being has been born. The human spirit longs for God but is afraid to find him. It is restless and unhappy without him, but fearful and guilty before him. That is the agony of fallen humanity.

The Invader

When the Spirit of God was withdrawn, the human spirit of Adam was left untenanted and unlighted. In this condition Adam would have been unable to move or even breathe, for God had supplied him the power to act. But though spiritually he was instantly cut off from God, physically he did not die, but was able to go on living, breathing, thinking, and working. By what power? The account in Genesis does not tell us, but centuries later Paul makes it clear. Adam was instantly invaded by an

alien power which took over the task of supplying the
energy and power he needed to fulfill his choices.
Adam was very likely only faintly aware of any
change in him at all. That alien power Paul described
vividly in his letter to the Ephesians:

> *And you he made alive, when you were dead
> through the trespasses and sins in which you once
> walked, following the course of this world, follow-
> ing the prince of the power of the air, the spirit that
> is now at work in the sons of disobedience (Ephe-
> sians 2:1-2).*

That power which operates universally in fallen man,
is, says Paul, in some way not understood by us, connected with and originates from Satan himself. He is
"the prince of the power of the air, the spirit that is
now at work in the sons of disobedience." The apostle
goes on to describe him as working out his effects
through what the Bible calls "the flesh."

> *Among these we all once lived in the passions of our
> flesh, following the desires of body and mind, and
> so we were by nature, **children of wrath**, like the
> rest of mankind* (Ephesians 2:3).

The emphasized words in the above passage make
clear that this alien invasion is a condition common
to all humanity. Since all men are sons of Adam by
natural birth, it is also clear that this passage is describing what happened to Adam in the moment of
his fall. James, in his general epistle, speaks also of a
wisdom which "is not such as comes down from
above, but is earthly, unspiritual, *devilish*" (James
3:15). And Jesus himself confirmed the fact that all
men are born into an evil condition when he said to
his disciples:

*If you then, **who are evil**, know how to give good
gifts to your children, how much more will the
heavenly Father give the Holy Spirit to those who
ask him! (Luke 11:13).*

The Tainted Fountain

When we think of the Devil and his relationship to
God, the Bible is most careful to make clear that
there are not two opposing gods, one evil and the
other good. The Devil, too, is a creature of God,
must live by means of the life he receives from God.
There is really only one source of life in all the universe, and ultimately every living creature or spirit
must derive its life from the one Author of Life, God
himself. But by some means not fully revealed, the
Devil has interposed himself between God and man
and takes the pure life (or love) of God and twists and
distorts it so that it is no longer outward directed, as
it came from God, but it becomes inward directed;
that is, no longer other-loving, but it becomes self-
loving. Fallen man thus receives the life of God as it
has been twisted and tainted by the Devil. That life is
called "the flesh." This, then, is the primary characteristic of the flesh: it is self-serving. It is God's life,
misused. Thus it can have all the outward appearance
of the life of God: loving, working, forgiving, creating, serving—but with an inward motive that is
aimed always and solely at the advancement of self. It
thus becomes the rival of God—another god!

This is why fallen man, working in the energy of
the flesh, can do many good deeds—good in the eyes
of himself and others around. But God does not see
them as good. He looks on the heart and not on the
outward appearance, therefore he knows they are
tainted right from the start. Thus Paul can say, "For

the mind of the flesh is hostile to God; it does not submit to God's law, indeed it cannot; and those who are in the flesh cannot please God" (Romans 8:6-8).

A Greater Glory

So we come out at the two splendors again. There is a certain attractiveness about the flesh, trying to be good. It makes strong appeal to many, but it is like the shine on Moses' face—a fading glory! But the glory of the new covenant is far greater. It derives from the activity of Jesus Christ at work within man—directly and without Satanic twist. Thus it is perfectly acceptable to God. It is a delight to him, for it is the activity of his well-beloved Son and will ever be characterized by his life: genuine love, faithful work, unreserved forgiveness, freshly creative, serving without calling attention to it. That is man as God intended man to be.

5
DEATH VERSUS LIFE

At the moment you read this sentence you are seeing, reading, and thinking either in the energy of the flesh or by the energy of the Holy Spirit. To use the figures Paul employs: You are either looking at the face of Moses or you are looking at the glory of God seen in the face of Jesus Christ. You may not be at all conscious of this, but, nevertheless, it is true. Furthermore, it would be equally true if you were a primitive savage who had never in all his life heard of either Moses or Jesus. Certainly it is highly unlikely that you would be reading this if you were such a savage, but the point is that no one anywhere lives or acts except by the old or new covenants. There are no

other choices. Even the primitive man, Paul argues
in Romans 2, finds the law of Moses written to some
degree in his heart or conscience, and all that he does
relates somehow to the law of his conscience.

The Fruit Betrays the Root

"Well," you may say, "if one is hardly conscious of
which face you are looking at in any given moment,
how can you know when you are in the flesh and when
you are in the Spirit?" The answer is: by what is produced in the life! The flesh invariably produces one
kind of life; the Spirit invariably produces another
kind. Jesus has this truth in mind when he says: "You
will know them by their fruits" (Matthew 7:20).

Before we go on to look at Paul's most helpful and
practical description of the two kinds of living, it
would be well to remind ourselves that until one becomes born again as a Christian, he has no choice but
to live by the flesh and produce the life of the flesh.
The "good" which may be in his life is but an imitation good which comes from the flesh's effort to fulfill
the law of God, and it is really no better in God's
sight than the evil which the flesh manifests. It is but
disguised evil. On the other hand, to be born again
only supplies the possibility of living in the Spirit; it
does not make it automatic. The true Christian can,
and often does, manifest the phony righteousness of
the flesh, though he can also (and does, as he learns to
live by faith) manifest the wholesome qualities of the
Spirit.

There is a remarkable series of four contrasts in
2 Corinthians 3:7-11 which Paul draws for us so we
can recognize the effects of trust in the flesh and of
trust in the Spirit in our daily lives. When we learn
how to recognize which force is at work within us,

then we shall be ready to learn what to do in order to change from the flesh to the Spirit.

Death or Life?

The first contrast Paul makes describes the immediate effect produced by both the flesh and the Spirit:

> *Now if the dispensation of death, carved in letters on stone, came with such splendor that the Israelites could not look at Moses' face because of its brightness, fading as this was, will not the dispensation of spirit be attended with greater splendor? (2 Corinthians 3:7-8).*

The flesh produces death, the Spirit produces life! Paul has already pointed it out in verse 6: ". . . the written code kills, but the Spirit gives life." One is a "dispensation of death," the other is a dispensation of "greater splendor," that is, life. The word "dispensation" is helpful if we understand it in its original sense: to dispense or produce. If we think of a dispensation as a period of time, it will be confusing to use the word here. In reality ministry would be a much better word. The Greek is *diakonia,* which is translated ministry or service. What is being dispensed in the ministry of the Spirit? It is life. To depend on everything coming from you, in response to the demand of the law, produces immediate death. To depend on everything coming from God produces immediate life.

The Living Death

To think of death in terms of a funeral, as the end of existence, is to miss the point of what he is saying here. What is death? It is essentially a negative term meaning the absence of life. When a doctor examines an injured man, he does not look for signs of death; he checks for the signs of life. If he does not find them, he knows the man is dead. Life produces its own distinctive marks; death is the absence of those marks. That being so, the question we must really ask is: What is life? What do we mean when we say, "Man, I'm really living"? Enjoyment, of course! Enjoyment is a part of life, as God intended life to be. Purpose, meaning, worth, fulfillment, these are all part of life. How about other qualities—joy, peace, love, friendship, power? Yes, that's what life is. The moment we have these qualities we are living. Surely Jesus meant this when he said, "I came that they may have life, and have it abundantly" (John 10:10). That is Life with a capital L. Life lived to the full—love, joy, peace, long-suffering, gentleness, goodness, faith, meekness, self-control. That's life!

In contrast then, what is death? It is the absence or opposite of those qualities of life. What is the absence of love? Hate. What is the absence of joy? Misery, weariness of spirit. Thus fear, frustration, boredom, worry, hostility, jealousy, malice, loneliness, depression, self-pity—these are all marks of the absence of life, therefore, they are forms of death. We do not need to wait till we die to experience these; they are part of our experience while we are yet living. They represent death in the midst of life.

The Source of Death

Where do these attitudes and passions come from? What is it that suddenly brings them into our experience, sometimes when we least expect them? Jesus helps us answer these questions. "Are grapes gathered from thorns, or figs from thistles? So, every sound tree bears good fruit, but the bad tree bears evil fruit. A sound tree cannot bear evil fruit, nor can a bad tree bear good fruit" (Matthew 7:16-17). We think these negative qualities in our experience come from passing moods or changing circumstances. Both Jesus and Paul say, no! They come from something deeper, something much more fundamental. They arise from a dependence on the old covenant, the "bad tree" which cannot produce good fruit. They reveal that we are unconsciously or consciously depending on "something coming from me" rather than "everything coming from God."

These negative feelings, then, reveal the flesh in action. Not the flesh in the blatant display of evil which we usually think of—drunkenness, rioting, adultery, etc.—but the flesh in those subtler displays which we often approve and even seek after: self-confidence, self-pity, self-assertion. This is why every biblical counselor learns to look beyond the immediate manifestation of hostility, depression, boredom, etc., to the cause which produces these. For instance, I have learned in my own life (and also by observing others) that depression is usually caused by some form of self-pity. I become depressed because I suffer some disappointment or rejection and this causes me to feel sorry for myself. I want to be made much of, I want someone to center attention on me, and this produces depression.

Where does loneliness come from? Most frequently from some form of self-ministry, taking care of myself only. That is why the cure for loneliness is Jesus' word: "Unless a grain of wheat falls into the earth and dies, it remains alone [that is the inevitable result of refusing to die—loneliness]; but if it dies, it bears much fruit" (John 12:24).

The presence of these marks of death gives us the clue as to when the old covenant is at work. Whenever these negative qualities are there, the old covenant is working, for that is what produces them. On the other hand, whenever the qualities of joy, trust, confidence, beauty, worth, and fulfillment are present, they come only from the new covenant. It is the Spirit of God who produces them. They can come from no other source.

The Glory of Death

Paul reminds us that there are two glories or splendors involved here. There is a certain glory about the "death" which the old covenant produces, but there is a greater glory about life. There is a certain attractiveness about the marks of death. We take a morbid pleasure in them. Have you ever caught yourself wallowing in a morass of self-pity and resisting all attempts to bring you out of it? You wanted to be let alone so you could have a good time feeling sorry for yourself. It gives a perverse feeling of pleasure. James says, "This wisdom is not such as comes down from above, but is earthly, unspiritual [the word is really sensual or pleasurable], devilish." He goes on immediately to add: "For where jealousy and selfish ambition exist, there will be disorder and every vile practice" (James 3:15-16). The amazing thing is that we prefer these temporary, fleeting pleasures to the glory which accompanies real life. Often we naïvely assume we can enjoy both. But if we insist on having the momentary pleasure that comes from the old covenant, then we cannot have the lasting pleasure that comes from the new covenant. "No man can serve two masters," remember? So the first contrast the apostle draws, by which we can recognize the old or new covenants in action, is that of the immediate effects produced in life.

Stones or Hearts

The second contrast is associated with the first. It has to do with the material substance with which each is concerned. In 2 Corinthians 3:3 the apostle has already referred to these differences. The new covenant, he says, is "written not with ink but with the Spirit of the living God, *not on tablets of stone but on human hearts.*" Twice in this passage he stresses the medium by which the old covenant came: "now if the dispensation of death, *carved in letters on stone,* came with such splendor . . ." The law was written on stones; the Spirit writes on human hearts. The old covenant is concerned with stones, things; the new is concerned with hearts, people.

One mark, therefore, of false Christianity is that it is always deeply concerned with the importance of things: stones, rituals, ceremonies, buildings, stained-glass windows, spires, organs, proper procedures. The emphasis is put on these at the expense of people. But when the new covenant is in operation, it is the other way around. People are the important matter. Things are only useful as they help or do not help people.

Look at Jesus. See how utterly careless he was about the minute regulations of the Pharisees when they stood in the way of healing people. Even the sabbath was set aside when it stood in the way of meeting the needs of a person. Jesus said that his disciples ate grain on the sabbath because the sabbath was made for man, not man for the sabbath. The ultimate concern of the new covenant is always for people. The old covenant puts things first.

A number of years ago, a church in California hired a young man to "reach youth and bring them into the

church." He was so successful that soon the au-
ditorium of the church was filled with young
people—but in the eyes of the church elders they
were the wrong ones, for they were for the most part
"street people" with bare feet, bizarre clothing, and
untraditional ways. Eventually the youth leader was
let go because, as he was told, "You are bringing this
trash from the streets into our nice sanctuary." That
is an extreme form of the old covenant in action.

The world of business and politics almost always
operates on the basis of the old covenant. That is why
money is usually more important than people. When
vested interests are at stake, the rights of people usually suffer. Let a company face a drop in sales or pro-
duction and what happens? Management takes the
axe and heads begin to roll with but little regard to
whether people are going to starve or not. Profits
come first. And how much of this attitude is also seen
in the church! Reputations often come before people.
Programs and customs are perpetuated, not because
they meet needs, but because status and acceptance
are at stake—a dead giveaway that dependence is on
"everything coming from us" rather than "everything
coming from God."

Guilt or Righteousness

A third contrast is found in 2 Corinthians 3:9,
marking the difference between freedom and guilt:
"For if there was splendor in the dispensation of condemnation, the dispensation of righteousness must
far exceed it in splendor."

Here is another mark of the old covenant in action.
It inevitably produces a sense of condemnation, or to
use a more modern term, guilt. But the new covenant
produces quite the reverse: The feeling engendered is
one of righteousness. Unfortunately, "righteousness"

is one of those great biblical words which is little understood today. Most of us think of it as "doing what is right," and certainly that is part of its meaning. But the essence of the term goes much deeper. Its basic idea is "being what is right." One *does* what is right, because one *is* right—that is the biblical idea of righteousness. Righteousness is the quality of being acceptable to and accepted by God—fully and without reserve. Perhaps we will get the sense of it better if we substitute the word "worth." The righteous man is the man who is valued. All his internal struggles are resolved. He is no longer troubled with guilt, inadequacy, or hostility. He does not struggle with himself to produce anything, for he knows he stands accepted before God, pleasing to God. Therefore he is free to act with respect to the situation in which he finds himself. He is able to reach out to others who hurt or are fearful or feel condemned because he himself is free from these things. To depend on "everything coming from God, nothing coming from me" produces that sense of worth. That is righteousness.

The Pressure to Perform

On the other hand, how many Christians live continually under a sense of condemnation? When the basis for our Christian activity is dependence on something coming from us (our personality, our willpower, our gifts, our money, our courage, etc.), then there is no escape from a sense of guilt, for we can never be certain when we have done enough! Around the world that basis of performance is driving Christians into frenetic activity that can result in nothing but sheer exhaustion. I was in an American city recently where a woman stood up and told how her performance was being challenged in her church, and

she confessed how inadequate she felt and how
threatened she was. She was almost in tears, feeling
she had not done enough for God, but she didn't
know what else to do. What a far cry this is from the
joyful word of Romans 8:1, "There is therefore now
no condemnation for those who are in Christ Jesus."
How much this woman needed to see that God already loved her as much as he ever will, and nothing
she could ever do, or not do, would change that fact.
To really believe that truth would make her free to
"do"—not in order to win acceptance, but because
she was already pleasing to God.

The frenzied activities of Christians have become a
joke. Someone has revised the old nursery rhyme to
read:

> *Mary had a little lamb,*
> *'Twas given her to keep;*
> *But then it joined the Baptist Church,*
> *And died for lack of sleep!*

Many churches judge their basis of success by the
number of activities they have going. For many, it
comes as a great shock to learn from the Scriptures
that it is possible for a church to be an utter failure before God and yet be occupied to the full every night of
the week—teaching the right doctrines and doing
the right things. On the other hand, a church whose
people are living by the new covenant can also be
fully occupied with many and varied activities. It is
not *that* which marks the success or failure of a
church. It is what the *source* of that activity is. Is it the
flesh, or the Spirit? Is it *my* background, *my* training,
my education, *my* personality? Or is it God—at work
in me through Jesus Christ?

Surpassing Glory

Remember, there is a certain glory about the activity of the flesh which attracts many. Dedicated activity always gives one a certain sense of worth—for awhile! It produces a kind of self-approval which is very pleasant to experience—for awhile. There is, says Paul, a "splendor in the dispensation of condemnation." But it is far surpassed by the splendor of the dispensation of righteousness. In fact, the apostle enlarges on this. He says, "Indeed, in this case, what once had splendor has come to have no splendor at all, because of the splendor that surpasses it" (2 Corinthians 3:10).

This is undoubtedly an oblique reference to his own experience which we have already traced in a previous chapter. The pleasure which he derived from his dependence upon his ancestry, his orthodoxy, his morality, and his activity soon came "to have no splendor at all because of the splendor that surpasses it." To trust in Jesus Christ, at work in him, as he describes it in Galatians 2:20, is to experience a sense of fulfillment and worth that is infinitely beyond anything he had ever experienced before. It was to be free! Little did he care what men thought of him, since he was so fully aware of what God thought of him—in Christ. Little did he care what appraisal men (even other Christians) might make of his ministry, since he fully understood that what Christ did through him would always be "not in vain, in the Lord."

Fading or Permanent?

The final contrast Paul draws relates closely to the previous one. He says, "For if what faded away came with splendor, what is permanent must have much more splendor." The contrast is clear. The old covenant produces that which fades away, but the new produces that which is permanent. When Moses came down from the mountain with his face aglow, he found that the glory faded. Relatively soon it disappeared completely, never to be recovered. But the glory of the face of Jesus never changes. Those who are expecting him to be at work through them in response to the demands that normal living makes upon them will experience *eternal* results. They will never fade or lose their value. They are treasure laid up in heaven—not upon earth.

Once again Paul reminds us of the attractiveness that accompanies dependence upon the flesh. Challenging people to rely upon their natural resources and abilities can often whip up a tremendous wave of excitement and enthusiasm. From such a meeting everyone goes home saying, "Wow, what a tremendous meeting! I can't wait to get started on this new program. This year we are going to make it." But every leader of experience knows what will happen. Soon the enthusiasm will begin to ebb (it might not last beyond the next morning!). Those who go around later to collect on some of the promises made will find that people have grown dull and apathetic. At any rate, by next year it must all be done over again, with new approaches and more powerful presentations, in order to stir up the same degree of excitement and commitment. Sound familiar? "But," someone argues, "that is just human nature. We humans are just made that way. It is only realism to take it into consideration and make plans to overcome such apathy repeatedly." This statement is true—it is human nature. But it is fallen human nature: in other words, the flesh!

Fresh and Unfading

But have you ever met anyone who has learned to function on the basis of the new covenant? They don't need repeated meetings to whip up their enthusiasm. After twenty-five years they're still just as fresh and vital on the same job as they were the day they started. Not long ago I met an old man who had been a missionary to the loggers in the back woods of British Columbia for forty years. Recently he had been retired by his mission, but his zeal and enthusiasm for the Lord's work were unflagging. He had never grown weary of his work, though he was often weary in it, and if the mission would let him, he wanted to go back to the woods again with confidence and courage, knowing that the Lord who worked through him was perfectly adequate for whatever would happen.

The new covenant refreshes the spirit continually. When the human spirit weakens in the face of continued demand (as it was meant that it should), it looks immediately to the God who dwells within and from that Fountain of Living Water takes vigor and vitality to meet even the routine demands before it with unflagging zeal. People who live on that basis are a delight to work with. They do not require continual encouragement, though they fully appreciate the kind words people say to them, for they know the secret of their activity is "nothing coming from me but everything from God." That is the permanent glory which never fades. The activity of the flesh is always a fading glory.

The Big Shove

With these four contrasts Paul seeks to impress us with the total inadequacy of the flesh, despite appearances, and the total adequacy of the Spirit, despite the evaluations of men, whether of ourselves or others. It is the energy of the flesh versus the power of the Spirit of life in Christ Jesus, as Paul puts it in Romans 8. If, as a Christian, you are seeking to live by your own resources rather than by the life of Jesus within you, you are like a man who goes down to buy a car and doesn't know that it comes equipped with a motor. Naturally, a man buying a car on that basis would have to push it home. When he gets there, he might invite his family out for a ride, so the wife gets in behind the wheel, the kids in the back seat, and he starts pushing from behind. At that point you might come along and ask, "How do you like your car?"

"Oh, it is a tremendous car. Look at the upholstery, and get an eyeful of this color, and, oh yes, listen to the horn—what a great horn this car has. But, I do find it rather exhausting! It goes downhill beautifully, but if there is even the slightest rise in the pavement, I find myself panting and struggling and groaning. It is very difficult to push it uphill."

"Well, my friend," you may say, "you do need help. You know, at our church we are having special meetings this week. Our speaker is speaking on the very subject you need to hear: 'How to Push a Car Successfully!' On Monday night he is going to show us how to push with the right shoulder. On Tuesday night he will illustrate the techniques of pushing with the left shoulder. On Wednesday night he has colored slides and an overhead projector to show us how to really get our back into the work and push. On Thursday night he has committees and workshops organized that will help us all push more effectively, and on Friday night there will be a great dedication service where we all come down in front to commit ourselves anew to the work of pushing cars.

If you come every night next week, you will know all there is to know about how to push a car successfully!"

Power Drive

That is exactly where much of Christianity is being lived today. We spend many hours seeking to teach people how to mobilize all their human resources and try harder to get the job done for God. But all we are mobilizing is the flesh. We seek to build up their confidence in the power of numbers, the hidden resources of the human spirit, and the possibilities of a determined will.

But if we really wanted to help the man who is pushing his car, we would say something like this. "Look, come around here in front." We would lift up the hood and say to him, "Do you see this iron thing with all the wiggles coming out of it? Do you know what that is? It's a motor. A power plant. The maker of this car knew you would have the problem that you've been having and so he designed a power plant that would enable you to go uphill as easily as downhill. When you learn several simple things about operating the motor, you will begin to experience the power. All you need do is to turn on this key and the motor will start. Then you pull down that lever and step on the pedal on the floor and away you go. You do the steering, but the motor supplies *all* the power. You don't have to push at all. Just sit back and you can go up the highest hills with as much ease and relaxation as if you were going downhill. You will even find it exhilarating to encounter very difficult driving conditions, but you don't need to worry for the motor is equal to whatever demand you make."

Now that is what authentic Christianity is all about. God knew that we human beings aren't adequate in ourselves to meet the demands life makes upon us so he supplied a power plant—the life of Jesus himself. It is perfectly adequate for the task. Our part is to learn to operate it correctly and then to make the choices necessary to steering. When we do, we experience the restfulness of activity in the strength of Another. That is, indeed, a surpassing glory.

Let's Get Going

Perhaps many of you feel that you would like to quit reading at this point. The truth you have already learned is so exhilarating that you are anxious to stop reading and start living. I don't blame you. The adventure of new covenant living is wonderful to experience. But you will note that the Apostle Paul does not let us go at this point. He has much more to say, and what he says is very necessary if we are to experience what God would have for us.

6
THE ENEMY
WITHIN

"Since we have such a hope, we are very bold!"
That is Paul's triumphant conclusion to his discussion of the two covenants at work in humanity.

Boldness! This is the inevitable result of trust in the new covenant—everything coming from God, nothing coming from me. Boldness and confidence, of course, are just what people everywhere are searching for. They instinctively know that effective action must issue from a confident spirit. Consequently, they try in a thousand ways to build up that confidence. But they are looking in the wrong place. There is a form of boldness they can find in themselves, but it will end as a fading glory.

True Boldness

But not Paul! He has found the secret of true boldness. His basis is different. It is a sure "hope"; a conviction that God is ready to work in him. All who trust this fact soon become noticeably bold. Because they are not trusting in themselves or in some effort they are making on behalf of God but on God himself, they can be supremely confident. And since success does not depend any longer on their dedication, their zeal, their wisdom, their background or training, then they can be very bold. It is God who will do it, and he can be depended upon not to fail—though he very well may take some unexpected route to accomplish his ends. Trust that God is capable to work in any given situation delivers completely from the fear of failure. Hence, boldness!

When Moses Was Afraid

But Paul immediately adds: ". . . not like Moses." On at least one occasion Moses was not bold—he was, indeed, the very opposite. He was fearful and threatened. Let's read what Paul says about him:

> *Since we have such a hope, we are very bold, not like Moses, who put a veil over his face so that the Israelites might not see the end of the fading splendor (2 Corinthians 3:12-13).*

Here we learn something about Moses which the Old Testament does not reveal. In the Old Testament account Moses was not aware of the shining of his face when he came down from Mt. Sinai. Naturally it didn't take him long to learn that something unusual was happening when people closed their eyes or shielded their faces in his presence. It actually became necessary for Moses to cover his face with a veil when he talked to people. There was nothing wrong with that. It was a perfectly proper action in view of the circumstances. But Moses soon knew something that the people of Israel didn't know. The glory was fading. At first Moses put the veil on every morning because of the brightness of his face. But as time passed and the brightness faded to nothing more than a dim glow, he still wore the veil each day.

Now Paul raises the question, Why? Why did Moses keep the veil on his face after the glory had faded? His answer is: because Moses was afraid. Afraid of what? Afraid that the Israelites would see that the glory had faded! He did not want them to see the end of the fading glory. The mark of his privilege and status before God was disappearing, and Moses did not want anyone to know it. So he did what millions have done since, he hid his faded glory behind a facade, a veil. He did not let anyone see what was really going on inside.

The Veil of Pride

It is clear that Paul means this veil over the face of Moses to be a symbol of a further activity of the flesh, for he finds the same veil still around in his own day. The Jews of his time were a continuing example.

> *But their {the Israelites} minds were hardened; for to this day, when they read the old covenant,* that same veil *remains unlifted, because only through Christ is it taken away. Yes, to this day whenever Moses is read a veil lies over their minds: but when a man turns to the Lord the veil is removed (2 Corinthians 3:14-16).*

When Moses brought the Ten Commandments down from the mountain, he read them to the people. Their immediate response was: "All that God says, we will do." The confidence and pride of the

flesh rose up to say, "We've got what it takes to do
everything you say, God. Don't worry about us. We
are your faithful people, and whatever you say, we
will do." The truth was, of course, that before the day
was over they had broken all ten of the commandments. They knew it, but they didn't want anyone
else to know. So they put up a facade. They covered
over their failure with religious ritual and convinced
themselves that that was all God wanted. That pride
which would not admit failure was the veil that hid
the end of the fading glory. They could not see the
death that was waiting at the end. And they could
not feel the frustration and defeat that would be
theirs when the flesh had finished its fatal work.

Fifteen hundred years after Moses Paul found the
same veil at work in Israel. The Jews of his day made
the same response to the demands of the law as their
forefathers had made at Mt. Sinai: "All that you say,
we will do!" Now, two thousand years after Paul the
same phenomenon is occurring. When some demand
is made upon the natural life, its response is, "All
right, I'll do it," or at least, "I'll try." Even in Christians, the confidence that they can do something for
God blinds their eyes to the end of the fading glory.
They believe that something good can be accomplished if they just give it the old college try. So
today that same veil remains unlifted.

False Fronts

Veils come in many forms today, but in essence
they are always the same: representing the image or
front we choose to project to others, behind which we
hide our real selves. They are always, therefore, a
form of pride and hypocrisy. We don't want people to
see our fading glory. Actually, we are reluctant to
admit it has happened even to ourselves. And by

wearing our veils long enough there is great danger that we will actually begin to believe that we are the kind of people we want everyone to believe we are. Then our hypocrisy becomes unnoticed by us and its perpetuation is assured. This is that subtle deceitfulness of the heart which Jeremiah saw so clearly and lamented: "The heart is deceitful above all things, and desperately corrupt; who can understand it?" (Jeremiah 17:9).

Yes, the veils we employ are unbelievably varied. Pride has a thousand faces. It is a master of disguise. C. S. Lewis has rightly said,

> *There is one vice of which no man in the world is free; which every one in the world loathes when he sees it in someone else; and of which hardly any people, except Christians, ever imagine that they are guilty themselves. . . . There is no fault which makes a man more unpopular, and no fault which we are more unconscious of in ourselves. And the more we have it ourselves, the more we dislike it in others. The vice I am talking of is Pride or Self-Conceit; and the virtue opposite to it, in Christian morals, is called Humility* (**Mere Christianity,** *p. 106*).

Double-Entry Bookkeeping

Yet despite the unpopularity which pride creates for us, these innocent appearing veils are so necessary to our ego support that we invent many clever ways to preserve them. One is to have a double entry system of names. When a form of pride appears in others, we have one name for it; when the same thing appears in us, we have a nicer name for it. Others have prejudices; we have convictions. Others are conceited; we have self-respect. Others garishly keep up with the

Joneses; we simply try to get ahead. Others blow up, or lose their tempers; we are seized with righteous indignation.

C. S. Lewis suggests that only Christians become aware of pride in themselves. Certainly it is true that most non-Christians, if they see pride in themselves at all, regard it as a virtue rather than a vice. But unfortunately, being a Christian does not guarantee easy recognition of all forms of pride. Christians are particularly susceptible to donning certain veils, especially those which appear to be forms of Christian virtue. Take false modesty, for example. I have long ago learned that when I hear some Christian say, "I'm only trying to serve the Lord in my own humble way," I'm probably talking to the proudest person in six counties around. St. Jerome warned: "Beware of the pride of humility." I once heard of a congregation that gave its pastor a medal for humility, but then took it away because he wore it! True humility, of course, is never aware of itself. It is most noteworthy that the greatest saints have been most aware of their pride. And the truly humble person would never see this virtue in himself. Any degree of pious cant is a dead giveaway of the presence of towering pride.

Veils Christians Wear

Then there is self-righteousness. This is a particularly noxious form of Christian pride. It seizes upon some biblical standard of conduct and takes pride in its own ability to measure up outwardly while conveniently overlooking any failure of the inner or thought life to conform. The end result is a smug, patronizing, and even nasty attitude toward anyone who does not meet the standard. This is the sin Jesus struck at most forcibly. He exposed it in the Pharisees and said that even the adulterers and the extortioners would enter the kingdom of heaven before them. It is the sin of the crusader who habitually mounts a white horse and rides out to combat any form of evil which he considers reprehensible. Self-righteousness is also the sin of the woman (or man) who nags another, for the nagger is focusing upon a single point of conduct and ignores the areas in her (or his) own life where a similar failure is occurring. Instinctively, we retreat behind this veil whenever failure or weakness is exposed in us. ("I may be weak there, but at least I don't do such-and-such.") We keep self-righteous veils always close at hand so they can be put on quickly to keep others from seeing the end of the fading glory.

Another common Christian veil is sensitivity or touchiness. Persons who are touchy or excessively sensitive are easily hurt by the words or actions of others. They must be handled with kid gloves lest they take offense. And when offended, they suffer agonies of spirit and tend to wallow in a morass of self-pity for hours, or even days, on end. Their explanation of such agony is always the "thoughtlessness" or "rudeness" of others, but in reality it is their own protest at not being given the attention or prominence which they're sure they deserve. Years ago a wise Christian woman summed it up for me in a brief statement I'll never forget. "I've learned," she said, "that sensitivity is nothing but selfishness." That helped greatly to free me from a struggle I was having with touchiness at the time.

More Cover-ups

An impatient spirit can be a veil to hide the reality of what we are. It is often manifested to indicate importance or busyness. It frequently appears as a mark of zeal or dedication. But to be easily irritated, to

frown readily, or reply sharply is a form of pride usually used to cover insecurity or a deep sense of in-
feriority. A self-justifying habit reveals something
similar. Those people who can't stand to be mis-
understood but are forever explaining their actions
are really saying, "I want you to think I'm perfect. Of
course, I know that the present situation does not let
me appear so, but if you will just let me explain, etc.,
etc." It is no wonder this habit is frequently associated with what is called perfectionism.

But perhaps the commonest veil employed by
Christians is remoteness: the practice of keeping feelings and attitudes completely to oneself, even with
friends or close relatives. Remoteness arises primarily
from fear—the fear of being known for what one is.
Often, though, it is described defensively as "reserve," "privacy," or "reticence." It is clearly a veil to
keep others from seeing a fading glory and is a direct
violation of such biblical commands as: "Confess your
sins one to another, and pray for one another that you
may be healed" (James 5:16); "Bear one another's
burdens, and so fulfil the law of Christ" (Galatians
6:2—How can another bear your burden if you don't
share it?); and the direct and repeated command of
Jesus, "Love one another" (John 15:12), which he
goes on to define as including, among other elements, the sharing of secrets (John 15:15). Paul tells
the Corinthian believers (in 2 Corinthians 6:11) that
he has opened his heart fully to them and exhorts
them: "In return—I speak as to children—widen
your hearts also" (2 Corinthians 6:13).

The Big Lie

It is apparent from the above examples that the
flesh, or natural life, likes nothing better than to hide

or disguise itself. We all tend to fear rejection if we are seen for what we are. The Satanic lie is that in order to be liked or accepted we must appear capable or successful. Therefore we either project capability (the extrovert) or we seek to hide our failure (the introvert). The new covenant offers the opposite. If we will admit our inadequacy, we can have God's adequacy, and all we have sought vainly to produce (confidence, success, impact, integrity, and reality) is *given* to us at the point of our inability. The key is to take away the veil.

A modern songwriter, John Fischer, has captured, with delicious humor, the tendency of evangelical Christians to wear veils. Enjoy a good laugh at your own expense.

Evangelical Veil Productions

*Evangelical Veil Productions! Pick one up at quite a
    reduction;
Got all kinds of shapes and sizes; Introductory bonus prizes!
Special quality, one-way see through; You can see them but
    they can't see you.
Never have to show yourself again!*

*Just released—A Moses model; Comes with shine in a
    plastic bottle,
It makes you look like you've just seen the Lord!
Just one daily application and you'll fool the congregation,
Guaranteed to last a whole week through.*

*Got a Back-from-the-Summer-Camp veil, with a
    Mountain-top look that'll never fail,
As long as you renew it every year.
Lots of special Jesus-freak files, every one comes with a
    permanent smile,*

One-way button, and a sticker for your car.
(Repeat first verse—then shout:
   YOU'RE PROTECTED!)

                              (Used by permission of author)

The Great Unveiling

How can these veils be removed? The answer is clearly stated by Paul in the Scripture passage we are considering. Twice he says it: ". . . only through Christ is it taken away," and ". . . when a man turns to the Lord, the veil is removed." Immediately the apostle goes on to tell us, "Now the Lord is the Spirit, and where the Spirit of the Lord is, there is freedom." Here is our first real key in moving from the old covenant to the new. The key is the Spirit. Some may be confused by Paul's word, ". . . only through Christ is it taken away." They may ask, "Are we to turn to the Spirit *or* to Christ, to have the veil removed?" The answer, of course, is that it makes no difference. In Scripture, the Holy Spirit is frequently called the Spirit of Christ. It is his divine task and joy to enter the life of those who believe in Jesus and continually release to them the very life of Jesus himself. Thus, to turn to the Spirit is also to turn to Christ. It is by means of the Spirit that we turn to Christ.

We must further see that in practical terms "to turn to the Spirit" means to have faith in the promise of the Spirit, to trust the word of God. It is to expect the Spirit to act in line with what he has said he will do. Specifically, the promise is to apply to our practical, daily lives the full value of both the death and the resurrection of Jesus. His death has cut us off from our old, natural life. ("We know that our old self was crucified with him so that the sinful body might be destroyed, and we might no longer be enslaved to sin," Romans 6:6.) When we agree with this word concerning the specific form of pride we are at the moment experiencing (that is, the particular veil we are hiding behind), we are immediately freed by the Spirit from its control. We have called the veil what God calls it, which is usually also what we call it when we find it in someone else. It can no longer be excused or justified—we repudiate it, and the fleeting pleasure it offers us. That is what it means to turn to the Spirit. As Paul describes it, ". . . if *by the Spirit* you put to death the deeds of the body, you will live" (Romans 8:13). Remember, "When a man turns to the Lord, the veil is removed, and the Lord is the Spirit."

Free to Live

The second function of the Spirit is to make real to us in practical terms the resurrection of Jesus, as well as his death. This is the second part of "turning to the Lord." The first act of the Spirit ends the reign of the old life over us; the second act releases to us the resurrected life of Jesus. That is what the Scripture calls "freedom"; "where the Spirit of the Lord is, there is freedom." ("But if we have died with Christ, we believe that we shall also live with him" Romans 6:8.) When by faith in that promise we have turned from the flesh with its lying promise of success and have trusted in the Lord Jesus, dwelling within us by his Spirit, to be ready to work the moment we choose to act, we have in very practical terms passed from the old covenant to the new. Nothing coming from us, everything coming from God! That is freedom.

The apostle goes on to describe this freedom in glorious terms: "And we all, with unveiled face, beholding the glory of the Lord, are being changed into his likeness from one degree of glory to another; for this comes from the Lord who is the Spirit" (2 Corinthians 2:18).

Note the "unveiled face." By faith in the promise of God (that is, by the Spirit) we have ceased to look at the face of Moses and are now beholding with full vision "the glory of God in the face of Jesus Christ." The veil is removed. Moses and the law are gone; only Jesus Christ fills the horizon of our life—for that precise moment. It is altogether possible that a minute or two later we may, like Peter walking on the water, take our eyes off the face of Jesus and begin to look once again at our circumstances and our limited resources. At that moment, of course, Moses and the law return. The *temptation* to do this is not the act, and we can find our faith sorely tested while still having it fixed upon the face of Jesus. But when we succumb to these pressures and begin to trust ourselves or other men, we are back in the old covenant, wearing a veil over our faces, and must repeat the whole process for deliverance.

God Is Not Angry

But let us not despair or feel condemned when this happens. Remember that God has already made full provision for failure in learning to live by the Spirit. He anticipates our struggles and our defeats and only expects us to recognize them as well and return immediately to the principle of the new covenant. God is not angry with us or upset because we have fallen. We are angry at ourselves, perhaps, but that only shows us more fully how much we were expecting something to come from us. We need but to thank God for letting us see what we were unwittingly trusting in and then resume our confidence that Jesus is at work in us as we take up the task at hand again.

Changed by Looking

This continual return to "beholding the glory of the Lord" is doing something to us, says Paul. More and more areas of our conscious experience (our soul) are coming under the full control of the Spirit, and we are therefore reflecting an increasing likeness to Jesus; we "are being changed into his likeness from one degree of glory to another." This is what we often call "Christian growth" or "growing in grace." It means that because of constant practice of the principle of the new covenant, it is increasingly easy to keep the eyes of the heart fixed on the face of Jesus. Gradually it feels more and more "natural" to walk in the Spirit and not in the flesh. The writer of Hebrews speaks of those "who have their faculties trained by practice to distinguish good from evil" (Hebrews 5:14). It is still possible, under sufficient provocation or allurement, to act in the flesh in any given relationship of life, but it is increasingly unlikely, for the heart is being "strengthened by grace" (Hebrews 13:9).

Though this gracious effect is occurring in certain areas of the conscious life, it has not yet conquered all the areas in which we live. "Glory," the glory of the life of Jesus, is becoming dominant in some areas, but in others the flesh still reigns triumphant and must be attacked and subdued by the Spirit so that another "degree of glory" may become evident. What is happening has often been pictured as a throne room in the heart, where at first Ego is seated upon the throne, and Christ (symbolized by the cross) is waiting to be given his rightful place of rule, as in A below.

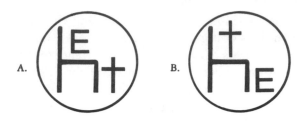

When the human will (the throne) is submitted to the authority of Christ, the Ego is cast off the throne and Christ rules as Lord in the heart, as in B above.

Growth Is a Process

This diagram has been helpful to many, but it is inadequate, for it represents the human heart as a single entity and the will as a single factor governing the whole of the inner life at one time. I believe it is more accurate to recognize the word "heart," commonly employed in Scripture, as referring to the soul and spirit combined, as in C.

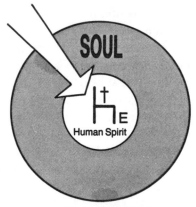

C. THE SPIRIT OF GOD PENETRATES
    THE HUMAN SPIRIT: EGO IS DETHRONED

Note in C that at the conversion of the individual the Spirit of God penetrated the human spirit, dethroned the Ego (or the flesh), and replaced it by the Cross, depicting the life of Jesus. But that was only within the human spirit. The soul is still under the control of the flesh and remains so until the Spirit successively invades each area or relationship and establishes the Lordship of Jesus within. There is, therefore, a throne in every area and the question of Lordship is fought out anew in each area, as indicated in D.

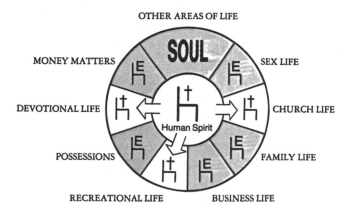

D. THE HOLY SPIRIT INVADES AREAS OF THE SOUL
  † = THE LORDSHIP OF CHRIST
  E = EGO, OR FLESH, IN CONTROL

The Up and Down Life

This would explain why it is possible for an individual Christian to be in the Spirit one moment and in the flesh the next. A good biblical example of this is in Matthew 16:16 where Peter confesses to Jesus, "You are the Christ, the Son of the living God." To this Jesus replies, "Blessed are you, Simon Bar-Jona!

For flesh and blood has not revealed this to you, but my Father who is in heaven." It is clear here that Peter spoke in the Spirit when he made his confession of the identity of Jesus. However, in verse 22 of the same account, Peter actually rebukes Jesus for suggesting that he will be crucified and resurrected again. To this rebuke Jesus says, "Get behind me, Satan! You are a hindrance to me; for you are not on the side of God, but of men." Here Peter speaks from the flesh in ignorant opposition to the will and purpose of God.

It is evident here that when it was a question of Peter's rational acceptance or rejection of the *identity* of Jesus, the Spirit had already successfully enthroned Jesus as Lord in that area of Peter's life. But when it came to the matter of Peter's *involvement* with the program of crucifixion and resurrection which that identity made necessary, the flesh was still very much in the ascendancy and Jesus was not yet Lord of that area. But that was all in the realm of Peter's soul (his conscious experience); in his human *spirit*, Jesus was Lord and had been ever since Peter responded to Jesus' call and entered into life.

The Struggle Within

It is quite possible then for you habitually to walk in the Spirit in one area of life—say your relations with Christian brothers and sisters—but perhaps the moment you are involved with a member of your family, you enter an area where the flesh is still unconquered and speech and attitudes are fleshly instead of Spirit-governed. This frequently happens with young Christians. From his vantage point in your human spirit the Spirit of God exerts steady and unyielding pressure upon the area of family relationships, often precipitating several crises, until the will submits in that area too, and Jesus is enthroned as Lord there. Thus another degree of likeness to Christ is achieved and another degree of glory manifested.

Perhaps it is the sex life which holds out against the control of the Spirit. Or it may be the vocational life. Many a businessman has learned to live in the Spirit on Sundays, but on Monday morning when he steps across the threshold of his office, he says, in effect, "Here I am in control. I have been trained to handle affairs here, and I don't need God's help. I know what is expected of me and I can handle things on my own." That, of course, is the old covenant in its purest form, and such a procedure will guarantee the presence in that businessman of many forms of death: depression, boredom, resentment, anxiety, tension, and so on.

Fighting a Battle Already Won

Since we can live only in one area of relationships of our life at any given moment, it is evident that we can be in a Spirit-controlled area one moment and in a flesh-dominated area the next. This is why we can be a great person to live with one minute—delightful, because we are in the Spirit—and then a moment later some familiar pattern to which we habitually relate in the flesh intrudes and we are right back in the old covenant and are harsh, nasty, or cruel. When we become aware of those feelings within, we know we will lose our Christian reputation if they are allowed to show, so we snatch an evangelical veil and hide the fading glory.

But how encouraging to know that the Spirit will never give up the battle. He seeks in a thousand ways to invade each separate relationship of the soul, and gradually he is doing so—sometimes faster, as we yield to him; sometimes very slowly, as we resist and

cling to our veils. The more we work and live with
the face of Jesus clearly in view, the more quickly we
find each area of our life being changed into his likeness. We cannot do that work. It is, as Paul says, all
"from the Lord who is the Spirit." He will never cease
the work he has begun.

7
THE ENEMY
WITHOUT

"Therefore," cries Paul, with that eternal optimism that marked his apostolic career, "having this ministry by the mercy of God, we do not lose heart!" In the original Greek the word translated "this" is very definitive; "this kind of a ministry" is the thought. The kind he refers to is that which he has just described: a ministry in the new covenant where all veils are removed by a repeated turning to the Lord, and where the Spirit within reveals the character of Christ in ever-increasing areas of life.

How can there be room for discouragement in that kind of a ministry? There will be failures, for the flesh is wily and elusive, but they need only be momentary

setbacks. In any case, they are never intended to produce condemnation, but, instead, each is a learning
experience designed to lead to restoration and renewed activity in the strength of the Lord. As we
have already seen, on the basis of the new covenant,
inner problems (of fear, tension, hostility, inadequacy, or shame) can be quickly handled; the individual is left free to concentrate on the ministry before him.

That ministry, whatever its form, will bear the
characteristic marks of the new covenant—simplicity, liberty, and effectiveness. Paul describes it in
these terms:

> *We have renounced disgraceful, underhanded
> ways; we refuse to practice cunning or to tamper
> with God's word, but by the open statement of the
> truth we would commend ourselves to every man's
> conscience in the sight of God (2 Corinthians 4:2).*

In line with the two-step walk in the Spirit which
we discussed in the last chapter, we have here also a
negative and positive description of a new covenant
ministry. First, the negative: "We have renounced
disgraceful, underhanded ways; we refuse to practice
cunning or to tamper with God's word." Once again
the first century sounds strangely like the twentieth.
In Paul's time there were men (and surely, women
too) who felt it necessary to produce instant and visible results in order to appear successful in their
ministry. It didn't matter whether the ministry was a
public or private one, success rested upon obtaining
some visible sign of achievement. Consequently,
they turned to what Paul calls "disgraceful, underhanded ways" to produce the desired results.

Things Nobody Needs

It is only necessary to note the similar activities of our own day to know specifically what these disgraceful tactics were. Undoubtedly they consisted of psychological gimmicks, pressure tactics, emotional pleas, heavy-handed demands—as we see all too frequently today. They would also include high-powered promotional campaigns, self-advertising posters and handouts, and the continual emphasis upon numbers as an indicator of success. There is, of course, a legitimate use of publicity for informational purposes, but promotion is something else again. It was Jesus who warned, "He who exalts himself shall be abased, but he who abases himself shall be exalted."

In straightforward fashion, Paul renounced all these psychological tricks to gain impressive results. Perhaps he had even practiced them himself in the days of his phariseeism, and even, for awhile, after he became a Christian. But no more. They were not needed for a "qualified minister of the new covenant." Furthermore, he refused to practice cunning, as evidently many others were doing in his day. The thought behind "cunning" is a readiness to try anything. It conveys the idea of being unprincipled, without morals or scruples. In these days of religious racketeers, it hardly requires any enlarging upon. It is simple expediency, justifying the means by the apparently good ends achieved.

A final state of dishonesty was reached by those who descended to actually tampering with the Word of God to obtain the appearance of success they desired. This was not, as we might think today, an altering of the text of the Bible. There were very few copies of the Scriptures available in the first century. It meant, rather, a twisting of the meaning of Scripture or a misapplication of truth—a pressing of it to unwarranted extremes. A case in point is that of Hymeneas and Philetus who taught that the resurrection was already past (2 Timothy 2:17-18). While they didn't deny the resurrection, they tampered with the Word of God by relegating the resurrection to the past. It was probably a result of teaching partial truth instead of the entire scope of revelation. Many of the newer cults emerging today are employing this tactic to the confusion and hurt of many. True, this all sounds biblical, but it is actually tampering with the Word of God by subtle and devious means.

No Boasting Needed

None of these approaches is needed in a new covenant ministry, Paul declares. They mark the very antithesis of it, and the appearance of any of them in a ministry would indicate the indulgence of the flesh. There are a thousand or more ways by which the flesh can seek to counterfeit the work of the Spirit, and they are all aimed at one point: the achieving of an appearance of "success," which can then be used to enhance the prestige or status of the persons concerned. Because these practices are so prevalent in our day (as they evidently were in the first century, too) many young, relatively immature Christians are caught up in them without realizing it. Since few voices are raised to challenge them, such practices are easily accepted as proper. But it is at this point that the Word of God must judge us all. As Paul says a little later in this same letter, " 'Let him who boasts, boast of the Lord', For it is not the man who commends himself that is accepted, but the man whom the Lord commends" (2 Corinthians 10:17-18).

The Way to Go

In stark contrast to the multiplicity of evil is the simplicity of truth. In a great positive declaration, the apostle describes his own practice and the practice of all who labor in the liberty and sweetness of the new covenant: ". . . but by the open statement of the truth we would commend ourselves to every man's conscience in the sight of God" (2 Corinthians 4:2b).

There is a precise and clear definition of a new covenant ministry as it would appear in any public manifestation. The method is single and invariable: "by the open statement of the truth." Nothing more is ever needed. The truth as it is in Jesus is so radical, so startling in its breadth of dimension, so universal, so relevant to human life everywhere that no psychological tricks are needed to prop it up and make it effective or interesting. It is the most captivating subject known, for it concerns man himself, and at his deepest levels.

The goal of Paul's proclamation is equally clear: "we would commend ourselves to every man's conscience." The conscience, as used here, is the will of the human spirit as contrasted to that more fluctuating and flexible entity, the will of the soul. It is what a man knows he "ought" to do, whether he always does it or not. It is the deep awareness within every person of what it takes to be the kind of person he or she admires and basically wants to be.

Right Before God

To appeal to the conscience, therefore, is to seek to capture the whole man: body, soul, and spirit—

mentally, emotionally, and volitionally. It does not aim at mere intellectual agreement and certainly not at a shallow emotional commitment. Rather, it seeks to impress the conscience that commitment to Jesus is right; that is, in line with reality, and the only way to true fulfillment. It does not, therefore, demand immediate and visible results, though it will welcome any that may come; it is content to allow time for the growth of the seed that is planted and recognizes that individuals can only properly respond to what they clearly perceive and understand.

Finally, this is to be done "in the sight of God." As we have seen, this means an awareness that God is watching all that is done, appraising it and seeking to correct it where needed. But the phrase suggests even more. Since the new covenant is "everything coming from God," it means also that the inner eye of the soul is looking to God for the supply of power and resource to make the ministry effective. The responsibility for results is placed squarely on God alone. This is what gives the spirit of the worker a sense of serenity and peace. He or she is free to be an instrument in God's hands. That is the new covenant ministry in its outreach to the world.

That Veil Again

At this point in Paul's letter the unpleasant realities of life intrude again. That is the glory of the gospel; it never deals merely with the ideal but with life as it is, "warts and all." Ideally, if God is responsible for results and is desirous that all men be saved, then whenever the gospel is preached or taught there should be many responses. But in actual practice, this is not always true. What about those times? To this implied question the apostle responds:

> *And even if our gospel is veiled, it is veiled only to those who are perishing. In their case the god of this world has blinded the minds of the unbelievers, to keep them from seeing the light of the gospel of the glory of Christ, who is the likeness of God (2 Corinthians 4:3-4).*

Once again the veil of pride appears in this discussion. The reference this time is not to the veils which evangelicals employ but to those used by worldly men and women when they are confronted with the good news about Jesus. Paul referred earlier to the phenomenon of being at the same time "life unto life" to some who hear his preaching and "death unto death" to others. The latter fail to see anything good in the "good news" because there is a veil lying over their minds. To them the gospel appears unrealistic, remote from real life, making its appeal only to those who have a streak of "religion" in them. But it is their outlook which is the illusion. As Paul puts it, "the god of this world [Satan] has blinded the minds of the unbelievers." As always, Satan uses pride to blind their eyes. They are so confident of their own ability to handle life, so sure that they have what it takes to solve their problems. To them, therefore, Jesus appears to be dispensable, hardly worth considering. They fail to see that he stands at the center of life and that all reality takes its content from him. To argue against him is to argue with the very power that makes it possible to argue at all. Jesus is Lord, whether men know it or not, and ultimately "every knee shall bow and every tongue shall confess that Jesus is Lord, to the glory of God the Father."

Don't Dodge Life

It is helpful to know just when this satanic blinding takes place. A superficial reading of the passage leaves the impression that the minds are blinded or veiled after they hear the gospel preached. They hear it and reject it and, as a consequence, their minds are blinded. That is the common way of understanding this passage. But Paul declares that the blinding is "to keep them from seeing the light of the gospel," therefore it occurs before the gospel is heard. They are called "unbelievers," not because they don't believe the gospel, but because there is something else they have not believed in even before the gospel was heard. What is that? It is *reality,* the way things really are. The god of this world has successfully accustomed them to live by illusions which they take to be reality. They are not willing to face life as it is. Men are turned away from truth long before they hear the gospel because *they won't handle life realistically.*

A common example of this is the way many people avoid the word "death." Death is an unpleasant subject and yet it is a stark, naked reality with which every one of us must ultimately wrestle. Watch how uncomfortable many people are at funerals and how they want the service to be as short as possible in order to return to the familiar illusions they regard as real. Instead of grappling with the fact of death and facing its implications in life right now (which might very well prepare them to believe the gospel when they hear it), they choose rather to run away and hide their heads in the sand until the inevitable encounter with death leaves them no way of escape.

Escapism can be seen in many other ways, as well. Most people do not like to see themselves as they really are. They choose to believe a more acceptable image of themselves, even though there may come moments of truth when they suddenly see themselves unveiled. Some people train themselves to avoid anything unpleasant or difficult, and so they find themselves unwittingly trapped by the god of this world into believing fantasies and treating illusions as though they were real. Such people are very difficult to reach with the gospel. To them it is often a fragrance of death unto death.

Eyes Wide Open

Yet, occasionally, one meets non-Christians who have been trained to face life realistically and not to run from difficult things. They are usually those who have had a considerable amount of self-discipline and are accustomed to taking orders from someone else. For example, soldiers and marines frequently fit this description. Upon hearing the gospel these kind of individuals often accept it immediately. To them Jesus "fits." They sense immediately that he is that missing center for which they have long been seeking. There is no veil over their eyes.

It is tragic, though, that those who fail to see the gospel as reality are turning away from the very thing they most desperately want to find. The center of the gospel is Christ, and Christ, as Paul tells us here, is the likeness of God. Therefore, what is lost to these people is the secret of godlikeness—and that is what men long for more than anything else. God is a totally independent being, having no need within himself for anyone or anything else, and yet, in love, giving himself freely to all his creatures. It is that same kind of independence which man craves—to him that is the essence of godlikeness and is why he is forever crying, "Let me be myself; I've gotta be me!"

How to Be Godlike

What man does not understand, in his veiled view of reality, is that such independence for men arises out of dependence. It is God's desire that people be godlike. He wants them to be independent of all other creatures or things in the universe precisely because they are totally dependent on him. It was no lie for Satan to say to Eve in the garden, "If you eat of this fruit you will become like God." It was very difficult for Eve to see anything wrong with that because, after all, that was what God wanted. He desires godlike people. This is apparent throughout Scripture. "What is man that thou art mindful of him? . . . Yet thou hast made him little less than God, and dost crown him with glory and honor" (Psalm 8:4-5). What Eve did not understand was that only through Christ is godlikeness possible. Paul will sing in 1 Timothy, "Great indeed is the mystery of godlikeness: He was manifested in the flesh . . ." (3:16). Godlikeness is, of course, the new covenant in action—"everything coming from God, nothing coming from me."

The Light Dawns

Well, what about these people whose minds are blinded? Are they hopeless? Is there no way to reach them in their darkness? Paul's answer to that is magnificent:

> For what we preach is not ourselves, but Jesus Christ as Lord, with ourselves as your servants for Jesus' sake. For it is the God who said, "Let light shine out of darkness," who has shone in our hearts to give the light of the knowledge of the glory of God in the face of Christ (2 Corinthians 4:5-6).

His argument is that the preaching of Jesus as Lord (the center and heart of all reality, the one in control of all events) is a message that is honored by God, and that God is a being of incredible power and authority. In fact, he is the one who at creation com-

manded the light to shine *out of* darkness. Notice, he
did not command the light to shine into the darkness—he literally commanded the darkness to produce light!

Now why are these people perishing? Their
minds, Paul said, are blinded; that is, they live in
darkness. They have already turned from the normal
way by which God proposes to save men—that is, by
an honest response to reality (Hebrews 11:6). But
their case is not hopeless, for the God whom Paul
preaches is able to call light out of darkness. Light
they must have, but if they reject the light of nature
and life, there is still the possibility that when they
hear the good news that Jesus is Lord, God will do a
creative act and call light *out of* their Stygian darkness. For this reason the Christian can always witness
in hope, knowing that a sovereign God will work in
resurrection power to call light out of darkness in
many hearts. Jesus knew this: "All that my Father has
given me shall come unto me."

Jesus Is Lord

Paul sees himself as one of these men. Before his
conversion experience he had been intent on pleasing
God, committed to this great objective and doing his
dedicated best to fulfill it, yet the darkness in which
he lived was so deep that when he saw and heard
Jesus, he could not recognize him as the Son of God
but thought him to be a usurper and a vagabond. But
on the road to Damascus he was suddenly overwhelmed with light. Out of the darkness of his bril-
liant mind the light shone and illuminated the darkness of his dedicated heart. There he experienced
what he had long sought—the knowledge of the
glory of God. To his utter amazement he found it
where he least expected: in the face of Jesus Christ.

God set aside young Saul's brilliance, his dedication, and his blameless morality as having done nothing to advance him on his search for reality. Suddenly it was all made clear—Jesus is Lord! Using that key, everything began to fall into place; the universe and life itself began to make sense. And best of all, Paul found himself fulfilled as a man. Jesus was real and was with him night and day. Courage and peace and power were his as a daily inheritance, enriching his life beyond all expectation. He had found the secret of godlikeness.

Because of his own experience the apostle is careful now to keep his preaching sharply focused on the only subject God will honor by calling light out of darkness—that is, "we preach not ourselves, but Jesus Christ as Lord, with ourselves as your servants for Jesus' sake." The danger in preaching is that all too often we offer ourselves as the remedy for man's need. We speak about the church or Christian education or the Christian way of life, when all the time what people need is Jesus. The church cannot save, a knowledge of Christian philosophy does not heal, doctrine without love puffs up—only Jesus is Lord, only he is absolutely essential to life. When he is encountered, all the other things will fall into their proper places.

A Servant Heart

In view of this, the role of the Christian is that of a servant. He is there to discover the needs of others and to do whatever his master tells him to do to meet those needs. He is, therefore, a servant "for Jesus' sake." He is never the servant of men, but he is Jesus' servant and therefore serves men. That is an important distinction. A friend of mine said, "I have always believed that I should be a bondservant to men. But the tragic error I made was that I became a servant of people. I felt obligated to respond favorably when anyone called and asked me to do something. Someone would say, 'I think you ought to do such and such,' and I would say, 'Right, I'd better do it.' Then five other people would tell me what they thought I should do. Suddenly I found myself in trouble because I couldn't do everything. But when I checked the life of Jesus, I found that he was a servant of the Father, not a servant of men. He submitted himself to the people whom the Father picked out. That set me free."

God always honors a message centered on the Lordship of Jesus, and which manifests a servant's heart to those whom he sets in your path. The god of this world is clever and subtle. He knows how to lead men into darkness without their being aware of what is happening. But the God of resurrection is more than his equal. He will honor the open statement of the truth with the light of the knowledge of the glory of God in the face of Jesus Christ.

8
POTS, PRESSURES, AND POWER

The miracle of regeneration has been described by the Apostle Paul as light, springing up suddenly from midnight darkness. Light makes no noise and cannot be touched or felt, but it is unmistakable. It not only can be seen, but it is that by which we see everything else. "That is what coming to Christ is like," says Paul, "it enlightens you by the knowledge of the glory of God."

But Christianity is more than conversion. It is, as we have seen, a total Life to be lived in the midst of this present world without evasion or defeat. It is opposed by the flesh within and the Devil without so that one thing is certain—it will not be easy! But though total Life isn't easy, it will be remarkable, as Paul makes clear in his description of Christian life beyond conversion: "But we have this treasure in earthen vessels, to show that the transcendent power belongs to God and not to us" (2 Corinthians 4:7).

Nothing but Pots

There are two particularly important factors in this verse: the description of basic humanity and the revelation of the intent of God. Paul first looks at the basic material with which God works, and he describes it as being a vessel—"We have this treasure in earthen vessels." This is not the only place in Scripture where this figure occurs. Perhaps you have never thought of yourself as a vessel, but it is a fundamental and essential concept of the biblical view of man.

What are vessels for? They are essentially containers made to hold something. The vessels in your home (pots, cups, bowls) are made to contain something, and when nothing is in them they are, of course, empty vessels. That is the significance of this verse of Scripture. It reminds us that we human beings were intended to contain something. We were designed to be pots, capable of holding something.

What were we made to contain? That is the alluring question which has set man on a quest for his own identity since time began. The startling answer of the Bible is that we are made to contain God! The glory of our humanity is that it was intended to hold the Almighty. Our humanity is designed to correspond to Deity. "The dwelling of God is with men; . . . he will wipe away every tear from their eyes . . ." (Revelation 21:3-4). That is the glory of humanity.

It is accurate to describe lives without God as "empty lives." That is exactly what they are—devoid of what they were meant to contain. Dr. Carl Jung has described the world today as suffering from "a neurosis of emptiness." The result is hollow men and women who display an outward shell of busyness and interest but within there is nothing but an echoing emptiness.

Some Are Cracked Pots

However, it is fascinating to discover that in this verse we are not just vessels, but we are "earthen vessels"—made from clay, very common material, which in itself has little value. There is nothing very pretentious about man by himself. Despite his vast possibilities and his specious claims to great wisdom and cleverness, man must face the humbling fact that he is directly responsible for the terrible problems that now throttle the earth. Apart from God, he is nothing but a humble earthen pot—and sometimes a cracked pot, at that!

Of course, there are all kinds of grades of clay. Some people are like fine china—they crack easily. While they have a very fine texture, it is nothing more than a form of clay. Others are more like sun-dried mud and crumble at the first rap. Some are tough and resilient by nature, and others are pliable and easily molded. But all are clay. Underneath, we are all ordinary people.

But the Christian is more than an empty vessel. He has something within—or better, Someone within. We have a treasure in the earthen vessel. And not only a treasure—a transcendent power! That is humanity as God intended it to be. The vessel is not much in itself, but it holds an inestimable treasure, beyond price, and a transcendent power, greater than any other power known to men.

Hidden Treasure

That is the second great truth found in this verse of Scripture. God has designed even ordinary people like us so that we may be the bearers of the most remarkable riches and power ever known. It must be apparent to all, however, that the treasure and the power are not from us, but from God. Does that not sound familiar? "Nothing coming from us; everything coming from God." The point is that God designed it this way; he intended that his great power, wisdom, and love should become visible in very ordinary and otherwise inconsequential people.

> *God chose what is foolish in the world to shame the wise, God chose what is weak in the world to shame the strong, God chose what is low and despised in the world, even things that are not, to bring to nothing things that are, so that no human being might boast in the presence of God (1 Corinthians 1:27-29).*

The tremendous thing about all this is that the apostle is not merely using beautiful imagery. He is speaking of hard realities, of something genuine and practical, not merely idealistic and visionary. There *is* an inestimable treasure in each believer; there *is* a power beyond all telling. Paul puts it in clear terms to the Colossians as he describes his ministry to them: "To them [the apostles] God chose to make known how great among the Gentiles are *the riches of the glory of this mystery,* which is *Christ in you,* the hope of glory" (Colossians 1:27).

The only hope we have of realizing, even in this present life, the glory God intended for us is to learn to draw upon the treasure within and be empowered by the power available. That treasure and that power are Christ, in you! So valuable is the treasure that the world would pay anything to get it. It is, as we have seen, the secret of human adequacy, and billions of dollars are poured out every week in a vain effort to identify this treasure and channel it into the normal affairs of life. "Christ in you" is the lost secret of humanity, but when the full implications of the secret are realized, a person's life is enriched far beyond the ability to declare it. That is what sent Paul around the world of his day declaring what he called "the unsearchable riches of Christ." To see lonely, selfish, empty individuals transformed slowly but surely into warm, loving, wholesome, and happy people is to become aware of why Paul describes Christ as "unsearchable riches."

Power That's Different

The great secret within is such a treasure because, first of all, it is a transcendent power. Transcendent means beyond the ordinary. It is a completely different form of power. So often, in our time, power is used to tear things apart, to blast, or explode, or crush. But transcendent power unites, gathers, harmonizes. It breaks down middle walls of partition and removes barriers. It does not make superficial, external adjustments, but works from within, producing permanent transformations. Do you know of any other power like that? It is absolutely unrivaled. There is nothing like it anywhere else. Many philosophies and teachings seek to imitate this, and for a time they may produce a credible imitation, but in the end they all prove to be cheap and shoddy imitations. They cannot stand the tests to which life as it really is will expose them. In the end only "Christ in you" endures.

By design God entrusts this secret to failing, faulty, weak, and sinful people so it will be clear that the power does not originate from us. It isn't the result of a strong personality or of a keen and finely honed mind or of good breeding and training. No, it arises solely from the presence of God in the heart. Our earthiness must be as apparent to others as the power is so that they may see that the secret is not *us* but God. That is why we must be transparent people, not hiding our weaknesses and failures, but honestly admitting them when they occur.

Headed for Trouble

To show how thoroughly practical all this is, the apostle goes on to describe the way it works in the nitty gritty of life: "We are afflicted in every way, but not crushed; perplexed, but not driven to despair; persecuted, but not forsaken; struck down, but not destroyed" (2 Corinthians 4:8-9).

There are all the pressures common to man—and all present in the life of a Christian. Undoubtedly, one of the greatest misconceptions held by many is that being a Christian means that life should suddenly smooth out, mysterious bridges will appear over all chasms, the winds of fate will be tempered, and all difficulties will disappear. No, Christianity is not membership in some red carpet club. All the problems and pressures of life remain, or are even intensified. Christians must face life in the raw, just as much as any pagan will. The purpose of the Christian life is not to escape dangers and difficulties but to demonstrate that they are handled in a different way. There must be trouble, or there can be no demonstration. Look at the four categories of trouble Paul describes.

Afflictions: "We are afflicted in every way." These

are the normal irritations of life which everyone faces—the bothersome, troublesome incidents which afflict us. The washing machine breaks down on Monday morning; it rains on your day off; the dog gets sick on the new carpet; your mother-in-law arrives unexpectedly for a long visit; the traffic is worse than usual; you flunk the exam you expected to pass. All these are normal afflictions. They are the buffetings of life which come to everyone. Christians are not exempted from them.

Perplexities: Even the apostles did not always know what to do. They were sometimes uncertain and found it difficult to make decisions, just like all the rest of us. Paul said he tried to go into Bithynia, but the Spirit would not allow him to do so. He intended to preach the gospel in the province of Asia, but was ultimately forbidden by the Holy Spirit (Acts 16). Even Jesus seems to fluctuate, telling his brothers he is not going up to the Feast, and later changing his mind and going (John 7). There will be many times of uncertainty in our lives, many occasions when we do not understand what to do or what to say. These are normal perplexities.

Persecutions: The Christian is promised persecutions. Even worldlings are often persecuted, but the Christian can count on it, for his Master was persecuted also. The word covers the entire range of intended offenses against Christians from slight ostracisms, cold shoulders, snide words, and critical remarks to deliberate efforts to hinder, personal and bodily attacks, and even torture and death. Christians can expect any or all of these. The apostles were persecuted unto death, as even the Lord was, and "the servant is no greater than his Master."

Catastrophes: "Struck down!" The word has power to chill the heart. It refers to the stunning, shattering blows which seem to come to us out of the blue—cancer, fatal accidents, a heart attack, riot, war, earthquakes, insanity. Christians are not always protected from these. They are terrible experiences which try faith to the limit and leave us frightened and baffled. The Book of Job is clear proof that these stunning catastrophes can occur to believers and that the loving heart of God is nevertheless behind them.

Behold the Difference

But look at the reactions to these trials which Paul describes. "Afflicted, *but not crushed!* Perplexed, *but not driven to despair!* Persecuted, *but not forsaken!* Struck down, *but not destroyed!*" There is a power within, a transcendent power, different from anything else, which keeps pushing back with greater pressure against whatever comes from without, so that we are not crushed, despairing, forsaken, or destroyed. This power within was given to us for the very purpose of handling the afflictions which are our lot. We are exposed to them in order that we might demonstrate a different reaction than one which would come from a person of the world. Our neighbors, watching us, will find us difficult to explain, and it is only when we baffle them that we are likely to impress them with the advantage our faith gives. There will be a quality about us which can only be explained in terms of God at work. It must be evident that the power belongs to God and not to us.

When we ask ourselves whether this actually *is* the reaction of Christians to the normal trials of life, we must hang our heads in shame. All too often we react exactly as the unbelievers around us, or possibly not as well. We lose our tempers at minor irritations, we grow pouty and sulky when we're not given the favored place, we resent the perplexities to which we are exposed, and grow bitter and sullen at the catastrophes we experience. In all this we reveal ourselves to be unbelieving believers. Our problem is, as we have seen before, that we either are ignorant of the way of escape or do not choose to use it because we desire to have *both* the pleasure of sin *and* the deliverance which comes from the transcendent power within. But this is not possible. No man can serve two masters.

The Switchover

Once again the apostle brings us the key. In a passage of infinite light and beauty he indicates the process of switching from the old covenant, with its built-in death, to the new covenant and its power and life. The process requires a certain invariable order:

> *Always carrying in the body the death of Jesus, so that the life of Jesus may also be manifested in our bodies. For while we live we are always being given up to death for Jesus' sake, so that the life of Jesus may be manifested in our mortal flesh (2 Corinthians 4:10-11).*

The life of Jesus, manifest in our mortal bodies, right now, in time, is what we need and want. There are two factors which can produce it. One is an inner attitude to which we must consent (verse 10). The other is an outward circumstance into which we are placed (verse 11). But the result is the same for each: "the life of Jesus, manifest in our mortal flesh." Not in our immortal flesh, some day in heaven, but now, when we need it, when we are under the gun, facing the afflictions, perplexities, persecutions, and catastrophes of life.

What is the secret? It is, first, "always carrying in the body the death of Jesus." That is the inner attitude to which we must consent. The key to experiencing the life of Jesus is our willingness to accept the implications of his death. We will not discover the glory of the treasure and power within us until we are ready to accept in practical terms the result of the dying of Jesus.

The Cross at Work

The death of Jesus was by means of the cross, and the cross had only one purpose. It was to bring to an end an evil man! Those who were crucified had no life in this world beyond that point. It may sound strange to us to apply the term "an evil man" to Jesus, but it must be remembered that a little further on in this very letter the apostle says, "For our sake he [God] made him [Jesus] to be sin . . ." Literally, he was *made sin.* He became what we are. When he became what we are (evil men), there was nothing else God could do except to put him to death. That is what God does with evil people; he puts them to death. Thus, in the cross of Christ, God took all that we are in Adam, all our natural life with its dreams and hopes and resources and brought it to a crashing end by the dying of Jesus.

The cross of Jesus put to death the proud ego within us. It wrote off as utterly worthless that faculty within us which wants to blow a trumpet whenever we do what we think is good, or which, when there is an opportunity to show off, makes us want to get in line. It sentences to death that inner desire which wants no one else to be as educated or as popular or as skillful or as beautiful as I. It is the thing within me which struggles to be at the center at all times and expresses itself in self-pity, self-indulgence, self-excuse, and self-assertion.

Not Up to Me

I must clearly understand that it is not up to me to put this natural life to death—*it has already been done.* I am only expected to agree with the rightness of that execution and stop trying to make it "live" again before God. When a son was promised to Abraham, he cried to God, "O that Ishmael might live in thy sight!" (Genesis 17:18). But God refused, for Isaac was the child of promise, not Ishmael. Abraham must learn that though Ishmael was permitted to exist, God would fulfill none of his promise of blessing through him. Only through Isaac would the blessing come.

Thus when I cease trying to justify and excuse the activities of the flesh and agree with God that it is rightfully under sentence of death, then I am fulfilling this figure of "always carrying in the body the dying of Jesus." If I welcome the cross and see that it has already put to death the flesh rising within me so that it can have no power over me, then I find myself able to say no to its cry for expression. I can then turn instead to the Lord Jesus with the full expectation that as I will to do what he tells me to do in these circumstances (love my enemies, flee youthful lusts, wait patiently for the Lord, etc., etc.), he will be at work in me to enable me to do it. Thus "the life of Jesus" will be manifest in my mortal life.

It is this necessity to agree with the implications of the cross in terms of actual experience which Jesus has in mind when he says, "If any man would come after me, let him deny himself and take up his cross and follow me" (Mark 8:34). Paul is saying exactly the same thing here. The key to the new life is the belief that the old has been rendered of no value whatsoever

by the cross. And throughout Scripture the order
never varies. First death, then life. Death is intended
to lead to resurrection. "If we have died with him, we
shall also be raised again with him." When we consent to death, then the life of Jesus can flow unhin-
dered from us. It is never the other way. We cannot
claim resurrection life first, and then by means of that
put the flesh to death. We must first bow to the cross,
then God will effect the resurrection.

Something Done to Us

The second factor which produces the life of Jesus
in us is: "While we live we are always being given up
to death for Jesus' sake." That sounds very much like
the first, but there is an important difference. The
first was an attitude within to which we must consent. It was stated in the active voice (always carrying
in the body the death of Jesus). The second is stated
in the passive voice, that is, it is something done to
us, not something we are to do. We have no choice in
this second matter. We are being given up to death.
This refers to those circumstances of trial and pressure into which God puts us to force us to abandon
trust in the flesh and lean wholly on the Spirit of
Christ.

The encouraging thing about this is to see that it is
impossible for a true believer in Jesus not to walk in
the Spirit at least some of the time. God will see to it
that the true believer is put in circumstances which
force him to do so. A case in point is the experience of
Peter walking on the water. When he first got out of
the boat and walked on the water to Jesus, it was by
his own choice, though the power to do so came from
the Lord. However when his gaze wandered and he
began to sink, it was a moment of desperation. It was
either look to Christ or perish. When he cried out in

terror, "Lord, save me," Jesus lifted him up and they walked back to the boat together. So God is forever putting us into situations where we are way over our depth and are forced to abandon hope in all human resources and cry out, "Lord, save me." It is this which Paul calls, "being given up to death for Jesus' sake."

A Veteran Shares

There is a perfect illustration of this in Paul's own experience, recorded in the first chapter of 2 Corinthians. He says,

> *For we do not want you to be ignorant, brethren, of the affliction we experienced in Asia; for we were so utterly, unbearably crushed that we despaired of life itself. Why, we felt that we had received **the sentence of death** (2 Corinthians 1:8-9a.).*

We do not know what this experience was which Paul describes. Perhaps it was the riot which broke out in Ephesus as recorded in Acts 19. At any rate it was something so threatening and so dangerous that Paul despaired of life itself. He felt he had received the sentence of death. He was, literally, "being given up to death for Jesus' sake." Notice, though how he goes on: "But that was to make us rely not on ourselves but on God who raises the dead" (2 Corinthians 1:9).

God put him through this trying circumstance to keep him from relying on his own resources. And this is said of an apostle who thoroughly knew and understood the operation of the new covenant. Even he needed this painful help from time to time to keep him from succumbing to the subtlety of the flesh and to enable him to trust the God who raises the dead, the God of resurrection power.

This is why pressures and problems arise in our

lives. The God who loves us is delivering us up to death in order that we might trust, not in happy circumstances or in pleasant surroundings, but in the Lord of life who lives within. In the Scriptures we learn the attitude we are to have which releases to us the life of Jesus. Through our circumstances we are forced to *experience* this so that the treasure within might enrich us and the power within demonstrate before a watching world a totally new and different way of life.

Walking Through Life

This two-step process, repeated over and over again, is what Scripture calls "walking in the Spirit." We are to believe in the death of the cross and then appropriate the power of the resurrection. The simplest way to put it is: repent and believe. Repent is changing one's mind about the value of the old life; believe is appropriating the value of the new. In Romans 6 Paul says, "Consider yourselves dead to sin" (step one) "and alive to God in Christ Jesus" (step two). In Ephesians he says, "Put off the old man" (step one), "and put on the new" (step two). These are not widely differing things; they are the same, but put in many different figures so that all will understand. A walk consists of two steps, one with each leg, repeated again and again. So the walk in the Spirit is achieved when every demand life makes on us is met by taking up the cross that we might experience the resurrection. It can happen dozens of times a day.

Members One of Another

All this has an effect far beyond one individual life. The apostle says to the Corinthians:

So death is at work in us, but life in you. Since we have the same spirit of faith as he had who wrote, "I believed, and so I spoke," we too believe, and so we speak, knowing that he who raised the Lord Jesus will raise us also with Jesus and bring us with you into his presence. For it is all for your sake, so that as grace extends to more and more people it may increase thanksgiving, to the glory of God (2 Corinthians 4:12-15).

This passage is a recognition that the glorious effects of the life of Jesus may not always be seen to the full in a single believer's life. Sometimes the death is felt by one, and the resulting life by another. Paul feels this is the case with him. "Death is at work in us, but life in you." The Corinthians were experiencing the benefit of the death to which he was daily being delivered. He was content with this, being willing to be sacrificed for their faith so that they might understand and grow in the grace of Christ. His quotation is from Psalm 116:10 where the writer speaks of being sorely afflicted and not knowing quite why, but he had nevertheless believed in God and so had spoken of deliverance even before it came, saying, "For thou hast delivered my soul from death, mine eyes from tears, and my feet from falling." Thus Paul, too, is confident that God will strengthen him along with the Corinthians and bring them all together into the fullness of glory.

The closing sentence in the passage above is a magnificent statement of the unity of believers as members of one another. What affects one affects all. But though there are suffering, death, and tears, yet it is all working together for good, and as the new covenant is understood by more and more believers, it will result in a great outburst of praise and thanksgiving to the glory of God. Who can help but praise a God who can bring joy out of sorrow, life out of death, and liberty out of bondage? That is the new way of life which the church is called upon to demonstrate before a watching world.

But even that is not the whole story. This present experience only points the way to something beyond, which is so breathtaking, so glorious, that the apostle is beggared for terms to describe it. We shall examine it in our next chapter.

9
TIME AND ETERNITY

Something more is coming! Everything in Scripture points to it and everything within us cries out for it. God's work with us is not finished in this life. We have already seen that authentic Christianity is far more than a "pie in the sky, by and by" religion. It is magnificently designed for life on earth, right now, with all its pressures and problems, its joys and tears. But there is yet more. The Apostle Paul sees it as additional ground for confidence and courage:

> *So we do not lose heart. Though our outer nature is wasting away, our inner nature is being renewed every day. For this slight momentary affliction is*

> *preparing for us an eternal weight of glory beyond all comparison, because we look not to the things that are seen but to the things that are unseen; for the things that are seen are transient, but the things that are unseen are eternal (2 Corinthians 4:16-18).*

He states plainly that what we are going through now is but getting us ready for something yet to come—something so glorious and so different from what we have known that it is "beyond all comparison." In the words of Robert Browning in "Rabbi Ben Ezra" centuries later, and yet in a way more true than Browning ever intended, Paul is saying:

> *Grow old along with me!*
> *The best is yet to be,*
> *The last of life,*
> *for which the first was made.*

This is the Christian hope. It is more than merely looking on to life beyond the grave. It declares that everything which happens to us in this life is directly related to what is coming—in fact, is getting us ready for it. Nothing, then, is purposeless or futile in our present experience. It is all necessary to the ultimate end.

The Increasing Beauty Within

The apostle suggests three aspects of our present experience as believers which indicate that something much greater is coming. First, the daily inner renewal which we experience. "Though our outer nature is wasting away, our inner nature is being renewed every day." The sharp contrast he draws is between the effects of aging upon the body, which point to lessening powers and approaching death, and the increase of wisdom and the mellowing of love which mark the spirit of one who walks with God.

There is a beauty about godly old age which youth knows nothing of. The spirit broadens and grows serene though the body trembles and feels increasing pain.

What is happening? The outer man is losing the battle; the strength of youth falters and fades, the night is coming on. But the inner man is reaching out to light, growing in strength and beauty; the day is at hand. This inner renewal is another way of describing the new covenant in action. "Everything coming from God, nothing from me." The law of sin and death is destroying the body; the law of the Spirit of life in Christ Jesus is renewing the spirit and also the soul "from one degree of glory to another." To see this happening in oneself or in another is to be convinced that something wonderful lies ahead.

Trials Hardly Worth Mentioning

Furthermore, the apostle stoutly declares that it is our very trials and hardships which actually produce the glory to come! "For this slight momentary affliction is preparing for us an eternal weight of glory beyond all comparison." Surely there is a twinkle in Paul's eye when he writes, "this slight momentary affliction," in view of what he at a later time describes.

Five times I have received at the hands of the Jews the forty lashes less one. Three times I have been beaten with rods, once I was stoned. Three times I have been shipwrecked; a night and a day I have been adrift at sea; on frequent journeys in danger from rivers, dangers from robbers, danger from my own people, danger from Gentiles, danger from false brethren; in toil and hardship, through many a sleepless night, in hunger and thirst, often without food, in cold and exposure (2 Corinthians 11:24-27).

That is what Paul calls "this slight momentary affliction." But he was not complaining. He made light of it simply because he was aware of something we often forget. He knew that these painful trials were actually preparing the "weight of glory" which was coming! Notice he does not say that these trials were preparing him for the glory. While that was true, it wasn't what he said here. The trials were creating the glory!

Perhaps this throws some light upon a strange statement which Jesus made to his disciples in the Upper Room. In saying that he was going away, he added, "I go to prepare a place for you" (John 14:2, KJV). This cryptic statement seems to suggest that heaven was not yet ready and needed some additional work before any guests arrived! But if we link it with the further explanation which Jesus gave them (". . . but if I go, I will send him [the Holy Spirit] to you" John 16:7), we have the strong suggestion that his way of preparing a place for them was to send the Holy Spirit to them. The Spirit, when he came, would give them the power to handle the pressures and pains of life ("afflicted, but not crushed . . . struck down, but not destroyed"), and in the mystery of redemption, transmute each trial into a corresponding glory. Thus, the trials were preparing the glory; the hardships were preparing "the place" for them. Jesus was doing it by means of the Spirit.

Valuable Chains

There is a moving story which comes out of the persecution of the Christians in the third and fourth centuries. One aged saint had spent many years in a dark and gloomy dungeon, bound by a great ball and chain. When the emperor Constantine ascended the throne, thousands of Christians were released from imprisonment, and among them this old man. Desiring to recompense him for his years of misery, the emperor commanded that the ball and chain be weighed and the old man given the equivalent weight in gold. Thus, the greater the weight of his chain, the greater was his reward when release came. But the reality Paul speaks of is even greater than this. He says the weight of glory will be beyond all comparison. The Greek expression is, literally, "abundance upon abundance." It is such an abundance that it constitutes a great "weight." We speak of the "weight of responsibility" not always as a burden but often as a challenge. Here is the great challenge of a weight of glory, offering indescribable opportunity to those for whom it is prepared.

It seems clear, then, that something tremendous is ahead. Not only does daily inner renewal suggest it, and our present affliction is preparing it, but the very nature of faith itself guarantees it. ". . . because we look not to the things that are seen but to the things that are unseen; for the things that are seen are transient, but the things that are unseen are eternal" (2 Corinthians 4:18). Paul's argument here is very simple. The visible things of this life are but transient manifestations of abiding realities which cannot now be seen. If the transient form can exist, surely the reality behind it exists. The truly important thing is not the passing form but the eternal reality; consequently, the important thing in life is not to adjust oneself to the changing form, but to relate always to the abiding truth. It is the argument of Hebrews 11: "By faith Abraham . . . looked forward to the city which has foundations, whose builder and maker is God." "By faith Moses . . . left Egypt, not being afraid of the anger of the king; for he endured as seeing him who is invisible."

The Best Is Yet to Be

Well, what *is* it, that is coming? Like a good chef, Paul has been whetting our appetites and stimulating our anticipation by veiled references to some breathtaking experience yet to come. But now he grows specific. In chapter five he describes the weight of glory in more explicit terms:

> *For we know that if the earthly tent we live in is destroyed, we have a building from God, a house not made with hands, eternal in the heavens. Here indeed we groan, and long to put on our heavenly dwelling, so that by putting it on we may not be found naked. For while we are still in this tent, we sigh with anxiety; not that we would be unclothed, but that we would be further clothed, so that what is mortal may be swallowed up by life (2 Corinthians 5:1-4).*

"A building from God" . . . "a house not made with hands" . . . "our heavenly dwelling"; what do these expressions refer to? They are obviously set in direct contrast to "the earthly tent we live in" which is clearly the present body of flesh and bones. But before we take a closer look at these phrases, note how definite and certain Paul is. See how he begins: "We know . . ." There is nothing uncertain about it at all.

Many today, as in the past, are trying to guess what lies beyond death. Some have supposed that the spirit of man departs, only to return in some reincarnation of life as another human being. The evidence used to support this is usually the testimony of certain persons (often given through a medium or in a hypnotic state) who apparently recall whole episodes from their previous existence. But it must be remembered that the Bible consistently warns of the existence of "lying spirits" or demons who have no compunctions about representing themselves to be the spirits of departed persons and who take delight in deceiving humans. Others have suggested that knowledge of such things is put beyond us, that the only proper approach to life is to view everything as tentative, nothing can be depended on for sure. But Jesus and the apostles never speak that way. Christ said that he came to tell us the truth, that we might know. The Apostle John underlines this point again and again, saying, "These things are written that you might *know."* So Paul says here, *we know* certain things about life beyond death.

Things We Really Know

Well, what do we know? First, says Paul, we know that we now live in an earthly tent. Twice he calls the present body a tent. Tents are usually temporary dwellings. Once I visited a family who lived in a tent in their yard while waiting for their new house to be finished. It wasn't very comfortable, but they were willing to put up with it until they could move into their real house. This is the case, Paul says, with Christians. They are living temporarily in tents.

Further, he says that in this tent we both groan and sigh. Do you ever listen to yourself when you get up in the morning? Do you ever groan? It is quite evident that the apostle is right, isn't it? There is the groan of daily experience. Perhaps the tent is beginning to sag. The cords are loosening and the pegs are growing wobbly. There may also be the sigh of expectancy. "We sigh with anxiety," says the apostle, "not that we would be unclothed, but that we would be further clothed." No one wishes to be disembodied (unclothed), but nevertheless, we do long sometimes for something more than this body offers. We feel its limitations. Have you ever said when invited to do something, "I wish I could; the spirit is willing but the flesh is weak"? That is the sigh of anxiety, longing to be further clothed.

The Heavenly House

In contrast to this temporary tent in which we now live, the apostle describes the permanent dwelling waiting for us when we die. It is "a building from God, a house not made with hands, eternal in the heavens." This is the indescribable "weight of glory" which is now being prepared for us by the trials and hardships we experience. If the present tent is our earthly body, then surely this permanent dwelling is the resurrection body, described in 1 Corinthians:

> So is it with the resurrection of the dead. What is sown is perishable, what is raised is imperishable. It is sown in dishonor, it is raised in glory. It is sown in weakness, it is raised in power. It is sown a physical body, it is raised a spiritual body. If there is a physical body, there is also a spiritual body (15:42-44).

If the apostle can describe our physical body as a tent, then it is surely fitting to describe the resurrection body as a house. A tent is temporary; a house is permanent. When we die, we will move from the temporary to the permanent; from the tent to the house, eternal in the heavens. This resurrection body is further described:

> For this perishable nature must put on the imperishable, and this mortal nature must put on immortality. When the perishable puts on the imperishable, and the mortal puts on immortality, then shall come to pass the saying that is written: "Death is swallowed up in victory" (1 Corinthians 15:53-54).

When we compare this passage with the one we are considering in 2 Corinthians 5, we note that the word for "clothed" ("that we would be further *clothed*") is exactly the same Greek word as the one translated "put on" in 1 Corinthians 15 ("this perishable must *put on* the imperishable"). This present perishable body of ours must be clothed with imperishable life, and this present mortal nature must be clothed with immortality. It is at that time, says Paul, that "death is swallowed up in victory." Compare that with the statement of 2 Corinthians 5, "that what is mortal may be swallowed up by life." The two passages are clearly parallel and the "house not made with hands" is the resurrection body of 1 Corinthians 15.

Is There a Temporary Tent?

But this poses a serious problem with some. They say, "Well, if 'the building of God' is the resurrection body, then what does a believer live in while he is waiting for the resurrection body? Resurrection won't occur till the second coming of Jesus. What about the saints who have died through the centuries? Their bodies have been placed in the grave and won't arise until the resurrection; what do they live in during the interim?"

To this problem three widely varying answers have been posed. One is that departed saints have no bodies until the resurrection. They are with the Lord but as disembodied spirits, incomplete until regaining their bodies at the resurrection. But this view ignores Paul's words, "[We] long to put on our heavenly dwelling so that by putting it on *we may not be found naked.*" And again, "We sigh with anxiety, *not that we would be unclothed,* but that we would be further clothed." Furthermore, the language of both

1 Corinthians 15 and 2 Corinthians 5 seems to imply an immediate donning of the resurrection body. There is no hint of any waiting period.

A second answer to the problem is that of soul sleep. This theory says that when a believer dies his soul remains asleep within the dead body. When the body is raised at the resurrection, the soul awakens. But because it has been asleep since death, it has no knowledge of the intervening time and no awareness of having been asleep. This concept solves the problem of the missing bodies but directly contravenes such Scriptures as the Lord's words to the thief on the cross, "Today shall you be with me, in Paradise," and Paul's declaration, "we would rather be away from the body and at home with the Lord" (2 Corinthians 5:8).

Still a third group proposes to solve the problem by suggesting that the "house not made with hands, eternal in the heavens," is not the resurrection body at all but an intermediate body which God gives the believer to live in until the resurrection. Presumably, at that time, the intermediate body is dissolved and only the resurrection body exists. But it is difficult to square that with the description, "eternal in the heavens." Such a view also destroys the parallelism of 2 Corinthians 5 and 1 Corinthians 15. Since there is no hint anywhere in Scripture of the existence of an intermediate body, the view seems hardly tenable.

The Problem Disappears

The problem these strange answers propose to solve is really no problem at all. It arises only when we insist on projecting the concepts of time into eternity. We constantly think of heaven as a continuation on a larger and perfect scale of life on earth. Locked into our world of space and time, we find it very difficult to imagine life proceeding on any other terms. But we must remember that time is time and eternity is eternity and never the twain shall meet. We experience something of the same difficulty in dealing with the mathematical concept of infinity. Many people imagine infinity to be a very large number, but it is not. The difference is that if you subtract 1 from a very large number, you have one less, but if you subtract 1 from infinity you still have infinity.

Dr. Arthur Custance, a Canadian scientist who is also a remarkable Bible scholar and author of a series of biblical-scientific studies called *Doorway Papers*, has written something very helpful on this:

> *The really important thing to notice is that Time stands in the same relation to Eternity, in one sense, as a large number does to infinity. There is one sense in which infinity includes a very large number, yet it is quite fundamentally different and independent of it. And by analogy, Eternity includes Time and yet is fundamentally something other. The reduction of Time until it gets smaller and smaller is still not Eternity. Nor do we reach Eternity by an extension of Time to great length. There is no direct pathway between Time and Eternity. They are different categories of experience. (Doorway Paper No. 37. Published by the author)*

The thing we must remember in dealing with this matter of life beyond death is that when time ends, eternity begins. They are not the same, and we must not make them the same. Time means that we are locked into a pattern of chronological sequence which we are helpless to break. For example, all human beings sharing the same room will experience an earthquake together. While there are varying feelings and reactions, everyone will feel the earthquake at the same time. But in eternity events do not follow a sequential pattern. There is no past or future, only the present NOW. Within that NOW all events happen. An individual will experience sequence, but only in relationship to himself, and events will occur to him on the basis of his spiritual readiness. No two individuals need, therefore, experience the same event just because they happen to be together.

When Time Ends

All this may sound quite confusing, and it is true it contains great elements of speculation. But let us return to the Scriptures and the problem of what happens to the believer when he dies. Holding firmly to the essential point that time and eternity are quite different, then when a believer steps out of time, he steps into eternity. What was perhaps a far-off distant event in time is suddenly present in eternity if one is spiritually prepared for it. Since the one great event for which the Spirit of God is now preparing believers here on earth is the coming of Jesus Christ for his own, that is the event which greets every believer when he dies. It may be decades or even centuries before it breaks into time, but this particular person is no longer in time. He is in eternity. He sees "the Lord coming with ten thousands of his saints," just as Enoch did when he was permitted a look into eternity, and at a time when he was the seventh from Adam and the population of the earth was very small (Jude 14).

Where the Ages Meet

But what is even more amazing is that in the experience of that believer he does not leave anyone behind. All his loved ones who know Christ are there too, including his Christian descendants who were not even born yet when he died! Since there is no past or future in heaven, this must be the case. Even those who, in time, stand beside his grave and weep and then go home to an empty house, are, in his experience, with him in glory. Dr. Custance carries this even further.

> *The experience of each saint is shared by all other saints, by those who have preceded and those who are to follow. For them all, all history, all intervening time between death and the Lord's return is suddenly annihilated so that each one finds to his amazement that Adam, too, is just dying and joining him on his way to meet the Lord: and Abraham and David, Isaiah and the Beloved John, Paul and Augustine, Hudson Taylor and you and I—all in one wonderful experience meeting the Lord in a single instant together, without precedence and without the slightest consciousness of delay, none being late and none too early.*
> *(Doorway Paper No. 37, p. 28)*

This truly astonishing quality of eternity is the reason Jesus could promise his disciples with absolute certainty, "And when I go and prepare a place for you, I will come again and will take you to myself, that where I am you may be also" (John 14:3). That promise not only applied to that generation of Christians, but would apply to all, directly and personally, through all the intervening centuries. This also explains the strange promise at the close of Hebrews 11. Speaking of Abraham, Moses, David, Jacob, Joseph, and others the writer says, "All these, though well attested by their faith, did not receive what was promised, since God had foreseen something better for us, that *apart from us they should not be made perfect*" (Hebrews 11:39-40).

To be "made perfect" is to be resurrected, so this passage specifically states that the saints of old will not be resurrected without us. Either they are disembodied spirits waiting for the resurrection (which we have already seen is not likely) or there is some way by which we can leave time one by one and yet participate together in one glorious experience of resurrection. The proper understanding of eternity supplies the answer.

Eternity Invades Time

There are other references in Scripture that present this same phenomenon of the apparent eclipse of time. For instance, in Revelation 13:8, Jesus is referred to as "the Lamb slain before the foundation of the world." Now the cross occurred at a precise moment of history. We know when the Lamb of God was slain. But the Bible says it occurred before the foundation of the world. How can an historical event which occurred at a certain spot on earth, in the biblical reckoning be said to have occurred before the earth was even made? The passage does not say that the Lamb was foreordained to be slain before the foundation of the world, but it says he was actually slain then. Surely it means that the cross was an eternal event, taking place both in time and eternity. In time, it is long past; in eternity, it forever occurs. So also would the resurrection, and in the same way, the second coming of Christ. When any Christian dies, he passes from the realm of time and space into timelessness, into the NOW of God when the full effect of these timeless events is experienced by him to whatever degree his spiritual state requires. But the Lord's return is an event yet to take place in historical time when the Church is complete and the end of the age has come. Perhaps this is the meaning of the Lord's words: "Truly, truly, I say to you, the hour is coming, *and now is,* when the dead will hear the voice of the Son of God, and those who hear will live" (John 5:25).

A problem passage for some, in this respect, has been Revelation 6:9-11 where John sees the souls of those who had been slain for the Word of God under the altar in heaven. They are crying out to God, "How long before thou wilt judge and avenge our blood on those who dwell upon the earth." In response they are told to be patient a little longer until the full count of martyrs is complete. This seems to indicate a sense of time in heaven and a need to wait for something in the future. How do we explain this in the light of what we have just seen regarding time and eternity? The explanation, of course, is that John, who sees all this, is still a man living in time and space on earth. It is necessary, therefore, that what he sees in heaven be communicated to him in the symbols and language of earth. This is a common phenomenon in the Book of Revelation. In the first chapter John sees Jesus in heaven. Does he really have long white hair and feet like burnished bronze and does a sharp sword come out of his mouth? No, clearly these are symbols which convey to John the power, wisdom, and glory of the Lord Jesus in his glorified, risen estate. The truth conveyed by the vision of the souls under the altar is evidently their identification with and concern for their brethren who are still on earth. They express themselves in terms of time and space in order that John (and we) may understand.

Can We Come Back?

Perhaps this also indicates a further condition of the eternal experience: those who have stepped out of time into eternity can, if they so choose, step back into time again, though remaining invisible. That is, of course, exactly what Jesus did repeatedly during his forty-day post-resurrection ministry. To those in eternity, time may be like a book on our library bookshelf. If we choose, we can pick up and browse through it at random. We can enter the time sequence found in the book at any place we desire, follow it through for as long as we like, and then lay it down to reenter (in consciousness) the time sequence in which we normally live. In similar fashion those in eternity may select some period of history which they would like to live through and step back into that time, living out its events, though invisibly. This, of course, is pure speculation and may not prove to be true at all, but it does at least fit the suggestion of Scripture that in a resurrected state we will be free from many of the limitations of our present body of flesh.

One thing is clear. Paul looked forward with keen anticipation to the day when he would put off his earthly tent and move into his heavenly dwelling. It would be, he says, a "spiritual" body, not meaning, as many have supposed, a body made up of spirit—something rather ethereal and immaterial—but rather a body fully subject to the spirit, designed expressly for the spirit. Now we must say, "The spirit is willing, but the flesh is weak." Then we can say, "My spirit is willing and the flesh is equal to its demands. Let's go!" Perhaps a quote from C. S. Lewis will help understand this point.

> *The command **Be ye perfect** is not idealistic gas. Nor is it a command to do the impossible. He is going to make us into creatures that can obey that command. He said (in the Bible) that we were "gods" and He is going to make good His words. If we let Him—for we can prevent Him, if we choose—He will make the feeblest and filthiest of*

us into a god or goddess, a dazzling, radiant, im-
mortal creature, pulsating all through with such
energy and joy and wisdom and love as we cannot
now imagine, a bright stainless mirror which re-
flects back to God perfectly (though, of course, on a
smaller scale) His own boundless power and de-
light and goodness. The process will be long and in
parts very painful; but that is what we are in for.
Nothing less. He meant what He said.
(Mere Christianity, p. 171)

Yes, something more is coming—something so different from anything we have known up to now that it defies description. Yet it is something so splendid and glorious that, even whispered, it sends chills of expectation down the spine of the universe. Phillips' verson of Romans 8:18-19 is beautifully expressive of this: "In my opinion whatever we may have to go through now is less than nothing compared with the magnificent future God has in store for us. The whole creation is on tiptoe to see the wonderful sight of the sons of God coming into their own."

The Courageous Life

Lest we become so enraptured with this splendid future that we lose all interest in the present, the apostle wisely reminds us that the key to this future is in our present exerience.

He who has prepared us for this very thing is God,
who has given us the Spirit as a guarantee. So we
are always of good courage; we know that while we
are at home in the body we are away from the Lord,
for we walk by faith, not by sight. We are of good
courage, and we would rather be away from the
body and at home with the Lord (2 Corinthians
5:5-8).

Twice in this passage Paul says that a clear view of the coming glory should mean that our present life is marked with good courage. Surely that means more than keeping a stiff upper lip. Rather, it means to be full of encouragement, to be joyful, expectant, confident. There are two reasons given for this. First, in preparing us for the glory to come God has given us the Holy Spirit as his guarantee. We do not need to doubt that the resurrection of our body is ahead, for the presence within us of the Spirit of resurrection makes it sure. Remember that in 2 Corinthians 4 the apostle says, "knowing that he who raised the Lord Jesus will raise us also with Jesus" (vs. 14). The Spirit knows how to resurrect dead bodies, for he has already done it once. Also, the Spirit has not only effected the resurrection of the body of Jesus but he has also been resurrecting our spirits every day since we became Christians. "Though our outer nature is wasting away, our inner nature is being renewed every day." How many times has the Spirit brought you back from a sense of death and darkness to renewed life, interest, and vitality? That power to renew is our guarantee that God will bring us to glory.

The Operative Principle

The second reason for confidence in the present hour is that though the resurrection life will be mind-blowing beyond description, it is nevertheless true that we are learning how to handle the resurrection body by the way we handle our present body now. Though resurrection will be something new, it will not be *entirely* new; even though it will be strange, it won't be *that* strange. Somewhere C. S. Lewis has said that these present bodies are given to us much as ponies are given to English schoolboys—to learn to ride "the ponies" in order to be ready for the glorious stallions that are even now arching their necks and pawing the floor in the heavenly stables.

What is it we are learning now that will be so necessary then? It is to walk by faith and not by sight! That is the operative principle of eternity, and we must learn it here. Certain hymns have reflected the idea that when we get to heaven we will no longer need to walk by faith but can then walk by sight. It is true that we will then "see" the Lord, but that in no way will eliminate our need to respond to him. In fact, it will increase it. Faith is the human response to a Divine offer. As we live by means of Christ now, by faith, so we will need to live by means of Christ then, by responding to his life and love.

At Home Now—At Home Then

It is for this reason that Paul uses the term "at home" to describe both our present experience in an earthly body and the coming experience when we are "with the Lord." We are now "at home" in the body, though away from the Lord. Then we shall be away from the body, but "at home" with the Lord. In either case, we are "at home." All our tenderest associations gather around the word "home." It is where we feel relaxed, at ease, natural. And when we step into the stunning glory awaiting us, we will feel the same way—at home, relaxed, at ease, because we have not changed our basic method of operation. At home, here in the body, we are learning to walk by faith in a way that feels natural, comfortable. At home with the Lord, it will be the same.

This was Paul's own experience in that strange episode he recounts for us in 2 Corinthians 12. There he says he was caught up in the third heaven, the very Paradise of God. But twice he says he did not know whether he was in the body or out of it. Though the experience was beyond description and he heard and saw things he could not utter, yet it was not unnatural. Paul was simply not aware of his body. He was too much at home to notice.

10
THE MOTIVES
THAT URGE US

"So whether we are at home or away, we make it our aim to please him" (2 Corinthians 5:9). Pleasing God is the proper occupation of the Christian both for time and eternity. We are learning to do it here; we shall perform it perfectly there. To please God always requires faith, for "without faith it is impossible to please him" (Hebrews 11:6). As we have already seen, to walk by faith is to live on the basis of the new covenant, continually accepting the judgment of the cross as to the flesh and choosing to act in dependence upon the resurrecting life of the Spirit. "We are the true circumcision," writes Paul to the Philippians, "who worship God in spirit, and glory in Christ

Jesus, and put no confidence in the flesh" (Philippians 3:3).

It is helpful to us to learn that the will of God which many Christians are seeking to fulfill is not so much concerned with *what* we do as it is with *how* we do it. God does direct us at times to certain activities or places, though often he will leave the choice up to us. But what he is continually concerned about is the resource we are counting upon for success in whatever we do. To depend upon "something coming from us" is to be displeasing to God, no matter what the activity may be. To do even a simple task (sweeping the floor, for instance), counting upon "everything coming from God" is to be infinitely pleasing to him. This is why Jesus was pleased with the widow's mite and with the offer of the loaves and fishes. Each of these incidents was a presenting of a simple object to God with the expection that he would do something with it. That is faith. That is what pleases God.

What Will Move Me?

But the real problem of the Christian life is not how to discover the will of God. That we have known, in one degree or another, all our lives. The real problem is to want to do it! It is the problem of motivation. That problem remains, even after we have discovered what it really is that God wants. I can know a great deal about the Christian life: I can know that the true purpose for my life is to please God; I can even know just what it is that will please him (faith); and I can remember in times past the pleasure it gave me to please God and the blessings which followed, and yet, confronted by the lure of the flesh, the pleasure of sin, and the ease with which it could all be justified (a veil), I can deliberately choose to disobey God. I have done it many times, and so have you! When the soul swings in the balance between truth and error, good and evil, what will tip the scale in the right direction? That is the real problem. It is the issue of motivation.

As with everything else in the Christian life, God has not left us without help at this point. There are two powerful forces which act upon us to stabilize our wavering wills and draw us back from the alluring brink. They are like motors to move us into right action. The word "motor" comes from the same root as motive. Now, to choose is our inherent human function, but to choose *rightly* demands that a force operate within us that will strongly incline us in the right direction. Paul describes these forces to us. The first, perhaps rather surprisingly, is fear.

> *For we must all appear before the judgment seat of Christ, so that each one may receive good or evil, according to what he has done in the body. Therefore, knowing the fear of the Lord, we persuade men; but what we are is known to God, and I hope it is known also to your conscience (2 Corinthians 5:10-11).*

Moved by Fear

Somehow the idea has grown among Christians that fear is an improper motive; that if it be accepted at all, it is base and inferior. But Scripture never takes that position. Everywhere, from Genesis to Revelation, and especially in Genesis and Revelation, the fear of the Lord is extolled as a very proper and highly desirable motive for living. In fact, it is regarded as foundational. "The fear of the Lord is the beginning of knowledge" (Proverbs 1:7). The psalmist exhorts us, "O fear the Lord, you his saints" (Psalm 34:9), and declares that a man reaches a stage of great danger when "there is no fear of God before his eyes" (Psalm 36:1). It should not surprise us, therefore, that Paul speaks first of fear when he sets before us the great motives of life.

But what comes to mind when we think of fearing God? Is it some abject, cringing, expression of terror like a dog crawling in fear to his offended master? Such fear is inspired by guilt, and guilt has absolutely no place in a believer's relationship to God. Well then, is it the fear which is born of hate which strikes back at God with defiance and anger when a divine demand is faced? No, hate, too, is no longer a viable motive in the life of a Christian. Then perhaps it is the fear that God will let us down—a lack of trust which makes the heart anxious and without peace. No, these are improper and unhealthy fears. The fear of which Paul speaks is something that is still there when a believer stands as a son before his loving Father, with a bold and confident spirit, making his requests known to him. It is a fear which finds its focus at the judgment seat of Christ.

This judgment tribunal is presented in Scripture as awaiting the believer when he steps out of time into eternity. "Therefore do not pronounce judgment before the time, before the Lord comes, who will bring to light the things now hidden in darkness and will disclose the purposes of the heart" (1 Corinthians 4:5). It is a time when "each one may receive good or evil, according to what he has done in the body." These verses seem to suggest that it is an occasion when the whole of our earthly life passes in review before us and we learn, often for the first time, what has been pleasing to God and what has not. It will undoubtedly be a time of great surprises. Many things we felt were acceptable to God and profitable to us will be found to be spoiled by improper motives or wrongful dependence—and many things which we had forgotten or believed to be insignificant will be honored of God as greatly pleasing to him.

The Secrets of the Heart

In line with what we have seen in the last chapter, there is a sense in which this judgment is going on in our lives right now. "If we judged ourselves truly, we should not be judged. But when we are judged by the Lord, we are chastened so that we may not be condemned along with the world" (1 Corinthians 11:31-32). Eternal life has already possessed our spirits and is gradually reclaiming our souls. Consequently, this judgment seat of Christ, which is part of eternity, has already begun. As we progress in the Christian life, we learn increasingly to understand that "what is exalted among men is an abomination in the sight of God" (Luke 16:15). Increasingly we judge ourselves on this basis. We learn to obey the words of Jesus to pray and fast and give alms in secret, knowing that the God who sees in secret will grant a reward, but if we do things "to be seen of men," we already have all the reward we will get.

Paul also speaks of this in 1 Corinthians 3:11-15:

> *For no other foundation can any one lay than that which is laid, which is Jesus Christ. Now if any one builds on the foundation with gold, silver, precious stones, wood, hay, straw—each man's work will become manifest; for the Day will disclose it, because it will be revealed with fire, and the fire will test what sort of work each one has done. If the work which any man has built on the foundation survives, he will receive a reward. If any man's work is burned up, he will suffer loss, though he himself will be saved, but only as through fire.*

Wood, hay, and straw are highly combustible and all grow from the earth—an apt figure for those works of the flesh which arise out of our natural life and are therefore rejected by God. Gold, silver, and costly stones, however, are noncombustible and, though found in the earth, are not a part of it—another apt figure, but this time of the deeds done of the Spirit which alone are able to survive this test of fire and are acceptable in the eyes of God.

The "fear of the Lord" which Paul connects with this sobering judgment comes from an awareness of the nature of God which realizes that he cannot be fooled or deceived in any way. It springs from the fact that God views us with stark and naked realism, and that since he is no respecter of persons, there is no way we can count upon privilege or favor for some special consideration before him. He is not swayed by our emotional pleas nor moved by our tears to change his evaluation. Our explanations and justifications made so easily before ourselves or other men will die un-uttered on our lips in the presence of Christ's immu-table majesty. His judgment will be inescapable and without appeal. Before the white light of those lov-ing eyes, all pretenses will fall away and we shall see ourselves as he has always seen us: "Then shall I know even as also I am known" (1 Corinthians 13:12 KJV).

Don't Waste It

It is this which motivates Paul to "persuade men." He does not wish to waste his life. He knows that with his keen mind, his strong and dominant person-ality, and his powers of persuasion he could easily achieve in the eyes of the world and many other Christians a most impressive record of influence and accomplishment. Doubtless he could easily become very wealthy or gain great prestige and fame. He had the natural gifts to take him to the top of whatever heap he should decide to climb. But what would it all mean at the judgment seat of Christ? Nothing! A sheer waste of time and effort! It would only be what Paul describes to the Galatians as "a good showing in the flesh," nothing but wood, hay, and stubble, consumed in a flash by the eternal fire of God.

To him, life is a great race, an endurance contest, which he is running, not against others but against himself. The goal he sees drawing ever nearer is his death or departure to be with Christ; the prize is the resurrection glory which awaits him there. The object of the race is to take each step in dependence upon the Spirit of God and not upon the energy of the flesh. "To me to live is Christ," is his passion. Once, after a Billy Graham crusade meeting, I slipped into a seat on a bus beside a young man who had gone forward in the meeting that night and given his heart to Christ. I spoke to him of what his new life would mean and, among other things, mentioned that he could now be free from all fear of death. He turned and looked me in the eye and said, truthfully I believe, "I have never been much afraid of death. But I'll tell you what I am afraid of—I'm afraid I'll waste my life." I believe that fear is deep within each of us. It has been put there by our Creator. No one wishes to waste his life. When we understand the terms by which the value of that life is measured, we find it to be a great force to help us choose the right and reject the wrong. "What we are is known to God, and I hope it is known also to your conscience." Thus Paul seeks to persuade the Corinthians to walk as he walked with the bright light of the judgment seat of Christ on his path.

The Supreme Motive

But there is something still greater than fear. A second force is at work in our lives which has power to move us even when the fear that we shall waste our lives leaves us unmoved, as sometimes it will. Paul now goes on to declare that greatest of all motives:

> *We are not commending ourselves to you again but giving you cause to be proud of us, so that you may be able to answer those who pride themselves on a man's position and not on his heart. For if we are beside ourselves, it is for God; if we are in our right mind, it is for you. For the love of Christ controls us, because we are convinced that one has died for all; therefore all have died. And he died for all, that those who live might live no longer for themselves but for him who for their sake died and was raised (2 Corinthians 5:12-15).*

Paul's behavior as a Christian was a source of bafflement to many at the church in Corinth. They could not understand his approach, and his motives were forever being questioned. He explains the reason for their perplexity in his first letter: "But I, brethren, could not address you as spiritual men, but as men of the flesh, as babes in Christ" (1 Corinthians 3:1). His actions seemed strange to them because they didn't understand the new covenant. They expected him to act and react to situations just as they did and were confused and baffled when he did not conform. It is clear from the above passage and others in the Corinthian letters that they expected him to boast of his exploits on behalf of Christ and to find subtle ways to commend himself before them, for this is what they did. But now he insists he is not doing this, though it might at first appear to be the case.

Rather, he explains that the force which prompts him to act contrary to the usual ways of the world is not arising from a secret ambition for position, but originates from Christ within: "The love of Christ controls [to press, to urge] us." Then he repeats to them some of the things they were saying about him. "For if we are beside ourselves, it is for God." This came in response to those who had suggested that his unexpected behavior was a product of madness, he was "beside himself." If that is the true origin of his actions, he suggests, at least it always had one object in view: It was for God. It, at least, lay in the right direction. Another group said, "No, he is in his right mind," and Paul responded "If we are in our right mind, it is for you." Again the objective was right, though they could not explain the actions. In each case, the goal could be anticipated when it was understood that the love of Christ urged Paul on. His actions were the actions of love, directed to the glory of God and the service of men, never for the advancement of self!

That is always highly suspicious behavior! The person who has no axe to grind, no angle for his own profit, is behaving singularly strange. The world expects that everyone will look out for himself: "Every man for himself, and the devil take the hindmost!" The world also knows that everyone who is smart hides his self-interest until the last possible moment. He always *appears* to be concerned for the welfare of others, though actually they know he is not. That is why one frequently hears, "O.K., what's your angle?" or "Now tell me what the catch is." Most Christians also reflect this view despite their high-sounding "God-words" in church.

Love Ever Gives

Therefore, to find someone who, observed over a long period of time and under various circumstances, behaves consistently contrary to this basic human principle, may cause some to be strangely troubled and perplexed. "Love is the explanation" says Paul. "It is the love of Christ which presses us, urges us on, takes hold of us and overpowers our natural self-interest, and makes us act contrary to nature." A death and a resurrection have occurred, he argues. "We are convinced that one has died for all; therefore all have died." When Christ became what we are, he died, and, therefore, we who are in Christ have died with him. The natural life has been shown to be worthless, totally unprofitable.

But there is more. "He died for all that those who live might live *no longer for themselves* but for him who for their sake died and was raised." If we died with him, we also rose with him, and the risen life we now live is different—it is no longer self-centered, loving itself supremely. It is outward-directed. It naturally and without self-consciousness reaches out to others—not a put-on but real. Whenever we yield to the love of Christ, says Paul, that is the way we act, and his love is the reason we act that way. Once we have yielded to that love we cannot help being self-giving, for that is the way love is. The love of Christ controls us.

An article which appeared in *Christianity Today* (June 21, 1974), written about Christians in the Soviet Union, contains a paragraph which beautifully illustrates this. A former criminal, Kozlov, later a church leader, writes of life in a Soviet prison:

> *Among the general despair, while prisoners like myself were cursing ourselves, the camp, the au-*

thorities; while we opened up our veins, or our stomachs, or hanged ourselves; the Christians (often with sentences of twenty to twenty-five years) did not despair. One could see Christ reflected in their faces. Their pure, upright life, deep faith and devotion to God, their gentleness and their wonderful manliness, became a shining example of real life for thousands.

That is authentic Christianity, whenever and wherever it appears.

A Trinity of Love

Some have raised the question, "When Paul says 'The love of Christ controls us,' what love is he referring to? Is it Christ's love for Paul, Paul's love for Christ, or Christ's love flowing out of Paul to others?" The question is a valid one, and we are not given much help from the Greek text. It will allow for any of the above meanings. But a verse in John's letter does help. It suggests where love begins. "In this is love, not that we loved God but that he loved us and sent his Son to be the expiation for our sins" (1 John 4:10). Love begins with God, not with us. Christ loved us first; even, says Paul in Romans 5, while we were yet sinners and enemies of God. His love for us, accepted by faith, awakens our love for him so that Peter can write, "Without having seen him you love him" (1 Peter 1:8). Paul agrees with this, "God's love has been poured out into hearts through the Holy Spirit which has been given to us" (Romans 5:5). When our hearts have been stirred and awakened by God's love, we are ready to reach out in love to our fellowmen, disregarding our own interests. "So, being affectionately desirous of you, we were ready to share with you not only the gospel of God but also our own selves, because you had become very dear to us" (1 Thessalonians 2:8).

It takes all three phases to fully manifest the love of Christ. But the important point to see is that love, not duty, is the proper motive for Christian functioning. "If you love me, you will keep my commandments" (John 14:15), says Jesus. It is not the other way around: "If you keep my commandments you will love me." This is also seen in Paul's frequent exhortations to very practical duties, "Husbands, love your wives," "Wives, submit to your husbands," "Masters, treat your servants justly and fairly," etc., but never without a reference to the motive that should urge them: "Out of reverence for Christ," "For the Lord's sake," "As unto the Lord." Love makes obedience easy; it is the delight of love to do what the loved one desires. Therefore, when the heart grows dull and obedience is difficult, the proper response of the Christian is not to grit his teeth and decide to tough it out but to remember who it is that asks this of him, and then for his sake to do it. When a Christian responds this way, he will find to his amazement that his own attitude has changed. A new outlook is born within him. That is what Paul describes in 2 Corinthians 5:16-17:

> *From now on, therefore, we regard no one from a human point of view; even though we once regarded Christ from a human point of view, we regard him thus no longer. Therefore, if any one is in Christ, he is a new creation; the old has passed away, behold, the new has come.*

Perhaps the clearest evidence that the new covenant is in operation is the change it makes in our view of others. No longer does position, caste, color, sex, or wealth matter. Everyone is seen to be of infinite worth because he is made in the image of God and can be redeemed through Christ. Nothing else really matters. Paul seems to suggest here that there was a time when he knew Christ "after the flesh." Does that mean that he heard Jesus teach and preach and perhaps had even met him? It seems likely that he had. If that is the case, a drastic change had occurred in his outlook.

The New View

A British Bible teacher and evangelist, Major Ian Thomas, has described that change so brilliantly that I want to reproduce it.

> *Paul, the Apostle says, "There was a time when, as Saul of Tarsus, I made my own reasonable estimate of this man called Jesus Christ, about whom I had heard so much. When I did so I wasn't unkind; I wasn't even prejudiced. I applied all the normal, reasonable methods of evaluation of my own day and I came to my own conclusions about Jesus Christ. This was what I found:*
>
> *"FAMILY BACKGROUND? A nobody! I had to agree with my theological colleagues that he was the illegitimate son of a faithless woman who was not only faithless but a liar.*
>
> *"FAMILY BREEDING? In common with all my comrades, I couldn't help coming to the conclusion that he was worth precisely nothing. He had absolutely no standing in his community.*
>
> *"PROFESSIONAL STANDING? I went into that pretty thoroughly. I discovered that he had no formal education; he was brought up in a peasant's home; he was an apprentice at a carpenter's bench; eventually he got through his apprenticeship and became a carpenter. In terms of*

professional status, I came to the reasonable, logical conclusion that he was worth absolutely nothing!

"THEOLOGICAL BACKGROUND? He professed to be a preacher, but I discovered that, by all reasonable human estimates, here again he amounted to nothing. He hadn't been to college; he hadn't been to seminary; he hadn't had any instruction whatever from the ecclesiastical dignitaries of our day; he had sat at nobody's feet. Professionally he was **nothing.** *He was but a tub-thumping rabble-rouser and an incorrigible street preacher. In terms of the ecclesiastical situation of my day and generation he was simply a nobody.*

"MONEY? He was born in a borrowed stable; when he wanted to give an illustration he even had to borrow a coin; he rode around on a borrowed donkey; when he wanted to celebrate the Passover he sent on a messenger and managed to persuade somebody to make his home available; he always lived in other people's homes. He was, on all the reasonable human basis upon which we can justifiably come to a conclusion, an incorrigible scrounger. He even died on a borrowed cross and was buried in a borrowed tomb. In terms of property or wealth he was worth absolutely **nothing.**

"But something happened to me, Saul of Tarsus, on the road to Damascus. Breathing out threatenings and slaughter, I was going to throw into jail and have put to death anyone who dared to perpetuate the myth that **this incorrigible nothing** *was the Christ of God.*

"Then, suddenly, there was a light brighter than the sun at noonday. I was blinded. I fell to my face. I was helpless. And I heard a voice, say-

ing, 'Saul, Saul, why do you persecute me?' 'Who are you, Lord?' I said. 'I am Jesus, whom you are persecuting.'

"*Then I learned that the one I had thought to be nothing, was NOTHING BUT GOD, MANIFEST IN THE FLESH. By my human evaluation he was nothing and as Saul of Tarsus I was everything. But on the road to Damascus I discovered that he became everything and I became nothing.*

"*Now I have such knowledge of him that I no longer know him from a human point of view which once I considered to be valid. Now, to me, to live is Christ.*" *(Used by permission.)*

Yes, life as a Christian is totally, radically, different. Impelled by the twin motives of the fear of God and the love of Christ, it goes counter to the normal impulses of life. It is that new creation, envisioned by the prophets, *already begun!* Right in the midst of the decay of the old creation the new is rising. Eternity is thrusting into time. Mastered by love, the Christian must continually swim against the current of his age until the day breaks and the shadows flee away.

11

THE GLORY
OF MINISTRY

The New Testament everywhere insists that the true Christian life is essentially and radically different from the natural life lived by a man or woman of the world. Outwardly, it can be very much the same: involved with making a living, going to school, getting married, raising children, mowing lawns, buying groceries, getting along with neighbors, and so on. But inwardly, the basis of living is dramatically different. Christ is a part of all these things! Life is lived by means of him. He is the motivator of every wholesome action, the corrector of every wrong deed or thought. He is the giver of every joy and the healer of every hurt. He is no longer on the circumference of life, acknowledged on Sunday but absent through the week. Christ is the center of everything. Life revolves around him. As a consequence, life comes into proper focus, a deep peace possesses the heart, strength grips the spirit despite outward trials, and kindness and joy radiate abroad. This is really living!

It is impossible to keep the secret of this kind of life to oneself. It cries out to be shared with others who are still struggling with guilt, despair, self-hate, and hostility. Whenever hurt is evident, sharing can begin. It has been beautifully and simply put as, "One beggar telling another where he can find bread." Sharing does not require a formal or stylized presentation nor a special place or time. It is not restricted to those who are ordained or are "in the ministry." Every person who has experienced true Christianity is already in the ministry because he or she possesses what others desperately need. It is this abundant ministry, available to all, which the apostle now describes.

> *All this is from God, who through Christ reconciled us to himself and gave us the ministry of reconciliation; that is, in Christ God was reconciling the world to himself, not counting their trespasses against them, and entrusting to us the message of reconciliation (2 Corinthians 5:18-19).*

Four times in this brief statement Paul stresses the word "reconciliation." Since man was designed to be indwelt by God, nothing could be more damaging to our humanity than to be estranged from the God who made us. Alienation from God is the fundamental sickness of humanity, and it breaks out in such hurtful expressions as guilt, hostility, and despair. Therefore the best news men could ever hear is that some means of reconciliation with God has been found. It is the great privilege of Christians to declare this good news to those by whom it is desperately needed and who are willing to listen because of the hurts and lacks of their own lives. Witness ought always to begin at the point of need. "Come unto me, all you that are weary and heavy laden," says Jesus, "and I will give you rest."

Certain elements of this ministry are underscored by the apostle to indicate its greatness and its relevance. To review these is to become aware of the inestimable privilege of proclaiming such a message to hurting and hurtful men and women.

It originates with God. "All this is from God," says Paul. The offended one is himself the one who initiates the way of reconciliation. The good news does not originate with man; it is not simply another of the many ways man has invented to try to find a way back to God. The very nature of the good news is such that it couldn't have been invented by man. It begins by postulating nothing in man except weakness, failure, and rebellion. By that one stroke, all competition is eliminated in the quest for salvation. No one can properly think of himself as any closer to God, apart from Christ, than anyone else. Those who pride themselves on their moral and respectable lives are no closer to God than the murderer or the sex pervert, for in reality pride of respectability is equally as much a manifestation of alienation from God as murder or debauchery.

This element of the good news is often highly antagonizing to many. Those who are counting upon what they imagine to be their good works are always deeply offended by this proclamation. They want God to take them on their terms. However, their offense is but further confirmation of the apostle's claim that "all this is from God." No flagrant sinner would dare to dream that he has some way to stand before God; no self-righteous person would dream that he needed anything to make him acceptable. Therefore, the good news of reconciliation could never originate with man. It comes wholly from God.

It is personally experienced. "God . . . through Christ reconciled us to himself." The Christian who witnesses to the new covenant does not speak academically. He is able to identify fully with the hurt and darkness of those to whom he speaks, for he has been there himself. But he has found something else, something so satisfying and complete as to make him eager to share it with others. He doesn't speak of "the plan of salvation" as though it were all theological doctrine, requiring only an intellectual grasp to experience it. Rather, he gives witness of a personal Lord who is at once the Savior and sustainer of his life. He does not convey the impression that when he surrendered to this Lord he was immediately and completely delivered from all struggle with evil, guilt, hate, and fear, but he makes it clear that the initial surrender produced a permanent change at the center of his being. And power continually flows from that center to enable him to conquer successively the areas of his life yet dominated by evil and failure. He freely acknowledges his present failures but rejoices in the certainty that they too shall succumb to the authority and power of a resurrected Lord. "Sin will have no dominion over you, since you are not under law but under grace" (Romans 6:14).

It is universally inclusive. "[God] gave us the ministry of reconciliation; that is, God was in Christ reconciling the world to himself." One of the wonders of true Christianity is its universality. It is not "the white man's religion," nor is it only for the blacks, the redmen, or the brown. It is not specially designed for the working classes any more than for the wealthy or those who live in ghettos. Men will find it speaking exactly to their need as men, and women will find it fulfilling and completing their femininity. It brings the wholeness of God to the whole need of every person physically, spiritually, and emotionally.

The silly idea has arisen somehow that Jesus is tender and compassionate toward lost mankind and stands between them and the Father—who is vengeful and angry—shielding them from the wrath of an angry God. Paul disposes of that concept forever with his clear statement, "God was in Christ, reconciling the world unto himself." It was the Father who initiated the work of redemption. It was he who sent the Son into the world to effect that redemption by his cruel death and subsequent resurrection. It was the Father who "did not spare his own Son, but gave him up for us all" (Romans 8:32). Therefore, it is the Father *and* the Son who, by means of the Spirit, reach out to a hurting, lonely world and offer pardon, peace, and joy to all who will come. No one is excluded by virtue of race, color, condition, or class. The door is wide open to all.

It is without condemnation. "Not counting their trespasses against them." Because of the cross of Jesus, the problem which human evil raises before God is totally eliminated. God does not require anything but the honest acknowledgment of evil to eliminate its baneful results in human experience. No penance is demanded or will be accepted. No self-chastisement is required. Any attempt to resort to

these is but proof that the individual has not believed
what God has plainly said. This is not only true when
a person first comes to Christ, but it remains true
throughout his entire life. The penalty of death for
any or all of my sins has already been fully borne by
Christ. And that means death in all its varied forms,
as we have been seeing. I only bear them in my experience when I refuse to believe God and seek in some
way to justify them before him. But the experience of
death ends the moment I believe him: "There is
therefore now no condemnation for those who are in
Christ Jesus" (Romans 8:1).

This is the element that especially makes reconciliation such good news. Acknowledgment of evil
with a consequent willingness to be delivered from
its power is all that God ever requires of us. The actual work of deliverance is accomplished by God for
us on the basis of the death of Jesus. The cross has *already* set us free; it is only waiting for us to believe
that to make it real in our experience.

We need to remember, of course, that certain
natural consequences of our evil will still remain in
our experience; sin will always leave its scars. But *they
will not work death to us, but life instead* by virtue of the
resurrection life of Jesus within us. "Blessed are those
who mourn, *for they shall be comforted*" (Matthew 5:4).
Thus the mistakes and rebellions of our past will be
turned into instruments of grace to mellow and soften
us and make us clearer and brighter manifestations of
God's redeeming love.

We need never hesitate to return to God when we
sin. He is already fully aware of it, expected it because he knows us better than we do, and is not angry
with us or ashamed of us. We may experience all
these emotions, but God does not. He has already
forgiven us and waits only for us to acknowledge our

misdeed and thank him for the restored relationship already ours.

It is personally delivered. "Entrusting to us the message of reconciliation." The good news does not come by means of angels. It is not announced from heaven by loud, impersonal voices. It doesn't even come by poring over dusty volumes from the past. In each generation it is delivered by living, breathing men and women who speak from their own experience. Incarnation, the word become flesh, is forever God's way of truly communicating with people. It comes always at the cost of hunger and thirst, personal hardship borne for Christ's sake—blood, sweat, and tears.

Some today have claimed to come to Christ apart from the aid of others, having read the good news in the Scriptures without the aid of teachers. But they have forgotten the labors and hardships endured by those who have given them the Scriptures in their own language, often at the cost of their lives. No one who reads the Bible in English ought ever to forget that Tyndale, Wycliffe, and Coverdale, the early translators, were all bitterly persecuted men who labored at the risk of their own necks.

It is easily demonstrable today that only a few Christians are able to read the Scriptures and grow by direct obedience to the precepts stated there. The rest of us seem to require models which we can follow. Only a few have the gift of faith which dares to challenge the accepted standards within the church which are biblically wrong. But when those few lead out and exemplify in their lives the consequent blessing, others are able to follow. Love must somehow become visible before it is caught by others. "We were ready to share with you not only the gospel of

God but also our own selves, because you had become very dear to us" (1 Thessalonians 2:8). There is a strong personal element about the gospel which cannot be eliminated without harm.

It is authoritatively accredited. "So we are ambassadors for Christ, God making his appeal through us." Ambassadors are the official spokesmen of a sovereign power in a foreign state. Their word is backed up by the power that sent them out, but only when the word of the ambassador truly represents the mind and will of the sending state. So Christians everywhere are authorized spokesmen for God, "God making his appeal through us," but only when they are living authentically as Christians. Whenever that is true, God honors their word by making visible and realistic changes in the lives of those who respond to their witness. It is the mark of *undeniable reality* which we saw in chapter two. In John 20:22-23 the risen Lord Jesus gave his apostles (and us, through them) the authority to declare the forgiveness of sins or the retention of sins, depending upon the response of listeners to the message of the gospel. To those who believe and accept, we may authoritatively declare, "Your sins are forgiven." To those who disbelieve, we have authority to say, "Your sins are yet retained."

This is part of that "priesthood of every believer" which Scripture teaches so clearly but which has been opposed by much of the institutional church through the centuries. Martin Lurther recoverd the truth briefly during the Reformation, but it was soon lost to sight again. Yet nothing is more encouraging to a servant of Christ than to see the Lord honoring his ministry by radical and permanent changes made in the lives of those whose lives he touches.

It is voluntarily accepted. "We beseech you on behalf of Christ, be reconciled to God." Throughout this passage the apostle uses words which underscore the noncoercive nature of the gospel: "appeal," "beseech," "entreat." Since, as he says, we make our appeal "on behalf of Christ" or, literally, "in place of Christ," it is important that we be no more coercive than Jesus was in the days of his flesh. In fact, authentic Christianity is Christ, by the Spirit, speaking through us yet today. It cannot be otherwise and still be of the Spirit. There is a remarkable absence of pressure in the presentations which Jesus made to people. He offers himself repeatedly to them; he invites them to respond; he warns them of the consequences if they refuse. But he does not harangue them or use emotional stories to sway them. When they seem reluctant to respond, he neither prolongs the occasion nor makes the invitation easier. In fact, he is forever sending men away and thinning the ranks of his disciples.

As we have already noted, the proper approach to the servant of Christ is by the open statement of truth to commend ourselves to every man's conscience in the sight of God. Appeal is made to the will to respond, and if it does not do so, the matter is left with God to work further in his will and time. This is true not only for the evangelist, but also for the pastor-teacher or anyone who imparts the truth of the new covenant. "A man convinced against his will is of the same opinion still." Truth must find a willing response from the heart or it is of no value. Contrived responses are a waste of time.

It achieves the impossible. "For our sake he made him to be sin, who knew no sin, so that in him we might become the righteousness of God." Here is the supreme glory of the new covenant. It actually achieves what could never be achieved by fallen man: righteousness (worth) before a holy God! It seems impossible even for God. How can a God of justice justify the unjust? How can a righteous God righteously declare a sinner to be righteous? It is a puzzle that staggers the angels. But it was achieved! He who knew no sin, Jesus the Righteous One, was made (on the cross) to be SIN on behalf of us, who knew no righteousness, in order that the righteousness of God might be forever OURS! Righteousness is not only our unchanging *standing* before a holy God; it is also our present *state* whenever we are walking in the Spirit. The cross, therefore, is forever the ground of Satan's defeat. It was the ace up God's sleeve which Satan could not have anticipated. The great accuser can never find any ground by which he can turn a righteous God against us, for *all* our evil was forever cut off from us in the cross, and we now have a totally new identity. We are one spirit with Jesus himself. "He who is united to the Lord becomes one spirit with him" (1 Corinthians 6:17). No wonder Paul shouts in Romans 8: "If God is for us, who is against us?" The inevitable outcome of righteousness is freedom. The righteous man is at rest; all his internal tensions and problems are solved. He is not anxious about himself but is free to give his attention to others. That is the glory of the new covenant. "If the Son makes you free, you will be free indeed" (John 8:36).

It is experienced moment-by-moment. The opening verses of chapter six are properly a part of the apostle's argument here:

> *Working together with him, then, we entreat you*
> *not to accept the grace of God in vain. For he says,*
> *"At the acceptable time I have listened to you, and*

> _helped you on the day of salvation." Behold, now is_
> _the acceptable time; behold, now is the day of sal-_
> _vation (2 Corinthians 6:1-2)._

It is possible to accept the grace of God in vain. That is, it is possible to live much of life in dependence on the resources of the flesh rather than on the power and riches of the Spirit. Then, of course, for such moments or hours or days Christ has profited us nothing. We have him, but we live as though he were not there. The grace and power of God are ours, but they do us no good.

Since we must take God's grace by faith (or dependence) and it comes to us moment-by-moment, then it is the present moment we must be concerned with. "Behold, NOW is the acceptable time; behold, NOW is the day of salvation." The fact that we walked in the Spirit a few moments ago is of no value to us now; the intention we have to walk in the Spirit in just a few more minutes does not redeem the present. If we choose to act in the flesh now, it is wasted time, gone forever, never to be retraced or regained.

Let us run the race of life seeking to live each moment in the power and grace of the Spirit of Christ, for any time spent in the flesh is time in which we have accepted the grace of God in vain.

This, then, is the ministry of reconciliation which has been entrusted to us by God. He does not send us forth alone, but goes with us himself to be both the Author and the Finisher of our faith. Perhaps it would help to summarize:

The Ministry of Reconciliation . . .
   Originates with God, not man
   Is personally experienced
   Is universally inclusive
   Is without condemnation

Is delivered by men
Is owned and accredited by God
Is voluntarily accepted
Achieves what otherwise is impossible
Is experienced moment-by-moment.

What a powerful and challenging opportunity His great ministry affords us! The apostle is himself caught up with the glory and wonder of it. He now closes this section of his letter dealing with the new covenant with a passage of infinite power and beauty in which his own experience of this ministry becomes Exhibit A.

12
EXHIBIT A

We began this book with Paul's great declaration of his own experience of the new covenant: "But thanks be to God, who in Christ always leads us in triumph, and through us spreads the fragrance of the knowledge of him everywhere." Now we have come full circle, for the words with which we close are taken from the sixth chapter and are, likewise, the apostle's own description of his experience in Christ. But there is a difference. At the beginning of this account Paul spoke in glowing terms of the great principles he had found in Christ which governed and empowered his life. But here, at the end, he speaks more specifically of deeds and experiences and final results.

How We Look to Others

This is as it should be, for principle must always work itself out into practice. "Faith apart from works," says James, "is dead" (James 2:26). Thus an understanding of the new covenant that does not drastically alter the way of life is a useless thing. Paul's primary concern in this final section is to address the problem of communication with others who do not yet know this great secret of godlikeness, whether they are new Christians or still unregenerate. The new covenant cannot be lived in isolation but must bring us into contact with others, both Christians and non-Christians, for authentic Christianity is designed for the world as it is. Therefore, the apostle says: "We put no obstacle in any one's way, so that no fault may be found with our ministry, but as servants of God we commend ourselves in every way" (2 Corinthians 6:3-4a).

There follows then a most remarkable list of very practical ways by which the new covenant may be commended to others. We shall look at this in some detail in a moment. But first, it may seem a contradiction for Paul to say here: "as servants of God we commend ourselves in every way," after he has said in 5:12, "We are not commending ourselves to you again." The commendation he speaks of in chapter 5 is that of words: boastful self-commendation which seeks to impress others. Here in chapter 6 it is the commendation of deeds and attitudes which speak for themselves.

We shall look now at this impressive list to discover the right way Christians can commend themselves and the teaching of the new covenant to others:

> . . . *through great endurance, in afflictions, hardships, calamities, beatings, imprisonments,*

> *tumults, labors, watching, hunger; by purity,*
> *knowledge, forbearance, kindness, the Holy*
> *Spirit, genuine love, truthful speech, and the power*
> *of God; with the weapons of righteousness for the*
> *right hand and for the left; in honor and dishonor,*
> *in ill repute and good repute (2 Corinthians 6:4b-*
> *8a).*

The translators have obscured, in part, the divisions which the apostle indicates in this paragraph. There are three major groupings of thought:

Through great endurance:
    in afflictions
    in hardships
    in calamities

    in beatings
    in imprisonments
    in tumults

    in labors
    in watchings
    in hunger
By means of:
    purity
    knowledge
    forbearance
    kindness

    the Holy Spirit
    genuine love
    truthful speech
    the power of God

With the weapons of righteousness:
    for the right hand and the left
    in honor and dishonor
    in ill repute and good repute

It is obvious that the first group deals with the adverse pressures which a Christian can encounter in life. The second group describes the character that must be displayed in the midst of these pressures. And the third group deals with the results produced, both good and apparently evil.

How fully Paul is the exemplification himself of all these things! The apostles were pattern Christians, chosen to experience the full range of pressures and possibilities in order that we might have in them (and supremely in the Lord Jesus) an example to follow. It is not likely that we will be called upon to endure *all* these experiences, but we will surely be asked to endure *some* of them. Let us remember that the world around is watching us and only the manifestation of what Paul lists here will commend us to them.

Endurance Which Endures

The key word to the first group is "endurance." It means far more than simply toughing it out. Even a non-Christian can endure hardness in that sense and some take great pride in their ability to do so. Athletes, marines, commandos, frontiersmen, and others often glory in their ability to confront hardship with fortitude and endurance. But this is not merely a reference to passive resignation which is content to wait with bowed head till the troubles have run their course. The Greek word used here, *hupomone,* goes far beyond that. Rather, it is the courageous triumph which takes all the pressure and emerges with a cheer! It not only refuses to be broken by the pressure but is actually grateful for the opportunity to endure, knowing it will bring glory to God. "Then they left the presence of the council, rejoicing that they were counted worthy to suffer dishonor for the Name" (Acts 5:41).

Paul endured triumphantly everything on his list, and often many times over. There were "afflictions" or, literally, "distresses." There were pressures that bore heavily upon his spirit, cares and anxieties that seldom seemed to ease. There were "hardships,"— the inescapable discomforts of life. And there were "calamities," or to be more exact, "strictures"; narrow places which seem to close one in on every side, offering no escape. In each of these circumstances the triumphant endurance produced by the new covenant would commend him to others.

More Troubles

Then there were troubles that stemmed directly from human opposition. There were "beatings" or "stripes." Further on in this letter Paul says, "Five times I have received at the hands of the Jews the forty lashes less one. Three times I have been beaten with rods; once I was stoned" (2 Corinthians 11:24, 25). These painful beatings left their scars upon him so that he could write to the Galatians, "Let no man trouble me; for I bear on my body the marks of Jesus" (Galatians 6:17). Often accompanying the beatings were "imprisonments." Clement of Rome tells us the apostle was put into prison seven times, though only four of these are recorded in the Scriptures. At least two imprisonments were for more than two years, so Paul spent at least five years in prison and perhaps much more.

But that was not all—there were also "tumults." This is a reference to the riots and mob violence which he sometimes provoked by the sweeping social changes which his preaching produced. Perhaps nothing is more frightening than an angry mob, out of control, bent upon venting its rage upon some hapless man. But amidst all of these encounters and hurts Paul was enabled to endure with triumphant courage.

The last category of events calling for endurance involved, first, the "labors" he assumed. The word he uses here describes hard, unremitting toil, to the point of exhaustion. Paul doubtless spent many long hours at his tentmaking in order to present his gospel without charge! There were also "watchings"—sleepless nights, spent in prayer and meditation. These were not a matter of mere convenience to Paul but required grace and commitment. Then there was "hunger." The reference is probably to periods of fasting, some deliberately chosen and some enforced upon him by the circumstances in which he found himself. These would take their toll of his physical and emotional strength, but through them all he was enabled to endure triumphantly.

The Secret Described

What was the secret of such endurance? It was never by a clenching of his fists, a jutting of his jaw, and a determination of his will to show the world how much he could take for Christ. Such an approach would soon have left even Paul broken and defeated, as he actually was in the early days of his Christian life. No, the secret of triumphant endurance was the new covenant—everything coming from God, nothing coming from me!

There was a certain kind of character he possessed which saw him through his troubles. It had to be invariable, or nearly so, for he never knew when it would be required. It consisted of four elements. First, there was "purity." This refers to the careful avoidance of all sin which defiles or stains the flesh or spirit. Paul never allowed himself to be found in a compromising relationship with anyone. He guarded his thought life with care, for he knew that is where defilement begins. Whenever he found himself toying with impurity, he immediately brought it to the Lord Jesus and obtained his cleansing and forgiveness. Next there was "knowledge." His mind was deliberately set upon truth, as he had learned it from the Scriptures and revelations of the Lord. He judged all persons and events, not from a human point of view, but from the Divine viewpoint as revealed by the Spirit. The doctrine of Scripture was always his guide. Third came "forbearance." The Greek word, *macrothumia*, means patience, especially with regard to people. By nature Paul was impatient and hard driving. But he learned by the Spirit to wait for others to catch up, to be understanding about their weaknesses, and to wait quietly for the Lord to do the work of correction that was needed, for "it is before his own master that he stands or falls" (Romans 14:4). Finally, there was "kindness." The original word has been described as meaning "the sympathetic kindliness or sweetness of temper which puts others at their ease and shrinks from giving pain." This attitude was to be shown without respect of persons, whether to a slave or to the emperor himself.

These four marks of Paul's character were what enabled him to endure. Anything other than momentary failure in any of them would have meant defeat. His pressures would have overwhelmed him, and he would have failed dismally to display that triumphant endurance which would commend him to the watching world.

Deeper Yet

But there was something deeper even than these. The four characteristics of purity, knowledge, forbearance, and kindness were visible to other people.

They lay in the realm of Paul's soul, his conscious experience in life. Deeper still, in the depths of his
spirit, were the forces that undergirded and kept on
making possible the display of the four characteristics
given.

Behind everything else and at the root of it all was
"the Holy Spirit." The Third Person of the Godhead
himself, the gift of both the Father and the Son, serving as the guarantee of all else to come, dwelling per-
manently in his heart, was the uncreated source of all
that sustained Paul. It was the Spirit's constant delight to release to Paul at all times "the life of Jesus."
Jesus himself, by the Spirit, lived in Paul and upheld
and empowered him, just as he proposes to live in us
and uphold us and empower us through all our trials
and tribulations. That "life of Jesus" invariably consists of three elements: love, truth, and power. Thus,
continually supplied to Paul, explaining all that he
was and did, was "genuine love," "truthful speech,"
and "the power of God." No wonder he could handle
life the way he did!

The Watchers

But Paul isn't through yet. Though the new covenant is designed to make us strong, it is so designed
in order that we might affect others. There is always that
watching world before which we must be commended! So Paul's final category speaks of the effect
of "the weapons of righteousness." He sees the worth
and value that he has in God's eyes (i.e., his righteousness in Christ) as a kind of sword or spear by
which the forces of darkness are assailed and men and
women held in bondage by Satan are set free. Hence,
the term "weapons of righteousness." Righteousness,
here, is a summary term gathering up the four dis-

tinctives that he had listed in the previous section: purity, knowledge, forbearance, and kindness. These four "weapons of righteousness" have a powerful effect upon others, but in a twofold way.

First, such righteousness affects both "the right hand and the left." This saying probably goes back to Jesus' statement in the Sermon on the Mount: "Do not let your left hand know what your right hand is doing" (Matthew 6:3). By that he refers to the public and private life. The right hand is the public life, the left hand is the private. Thus, the effect of a righteous life will touch both the public actions of others (their social relationships) and their private lives as well (changing their attitudes). True Christianity does not make superficial changes—it changes men within and without. Second, the effect of such change is also twofold: "in honor and dishonor." Those freed by Christ will be placed in varying positions before the world. Some will occupy positions of honor, such as Manaen, a member of the court of Herod, the tetrarch, mentioned in Acts 13, and Sergius Paulus, the converted Roman proconsul described in the same chapter. Others will be obscure men and women about whom the world knows or cares nothing. But even these will find a varying acceptance. Some will be "in ill repute" and others will be held "in good repute." Jesus himself had predicted this: "If they persecuted me, they will persecute you; if they kept my word, they will keep yours also" (John 15:20). But, whether honored by the world, or dishonored; whether held in good or ill repute, all are equally loved and owned by God, all are equally empowered by the Spirit if they choose to draw upon him, and all are expected to live before the world in such a way as to commend the gospel to it.

The Paradoxical Man

In this last characterization Paul moves to a final magnificent description of the Christian living authentically before the world. He will inevitably be to many an enigma because his life consists of a series of paradoxes.

> *We are treated as imposters, and yet are true; as unknown, and yet well known; as dying, and behold we live; as punished, and yet not killed; as sorrowful, yet always rejoicing; as poor, yet making many rich; as having nothing, and yet possessing everything (2 Corinthians 6:8b-10).*

These words scarcely require exposition. They are beautifully clear just as they stand. But only the man or woman who stands poised between two worlds can qualify for such a description. There he or she will be highly vulnerable, stretched between God and man. We must be content to be called an imposter by some, to be thought of as unknown, to seem constantly threatened and punished, to be poor and have nothing, yet knowing that before God the very reverse is true. As God sees us, we are his true children, known to all heaven, living and rejoicing in the spirit when the flesh is perishing, ever imparting the unsearchable riches of Christ to many, and being heirs of all creation when time trembles into eternity.

Open Up Your Lives!

Is it not fitting, therefore, that the apostle should close this great discourse with an earnest appeal, rising out of the depths of his heart:

> *Our mouth is open to you, Corinthians; our heart is wide. You are not restricted by us, but you are restricted in your own affections. In return—I speak*

as to children—widen your hearts also (2 Corin-
thians 6:11-13).

Love, truth, and power all require response to be
fully operative. Each will grow to infinite expansion
if it is met by faith, though it be as small as a grain of
mustard seed. The Corinthians were not being held
back by Paul. He had opened his heart to them and
told them everything he had learned from the Lord.
Their present weakness was due only to one thing: a
failure to respond to the truth they knew—a reluc-
tance to act on what they had been told. So his appeal
comes as a father to his children: "Widen your
hearts!"

The present low state of the church in the world is
surely due to the same cause. Christians do not really
believe what they sing about and profess. They have
lost the consciousness of the greatness of God and his
ability to act today. Dr. D. Martyn Lloyd-Jones,
noted pastor of Westminster Chapel in London,
England, has made an appeal similar to that of Paul's:

> *I speak especially to those of us who are Evangeli-*
> *cals. We must not continue with our religious life*
> *and methods precisely as if nothing were happening*
> *round and about us, and as if we were still living*
> *in the spacious days of peace. We have loved certain*
> *methods. And how delightful they were! What*
> *could be more enjoyable than to have and to enjoy*
> *our religion in the form with which we have for so*
> *long been familiar? How enjoyable just to sit and*
> *listen. What an intellectual and perhaps also emo-*
> *tional and artistic treat.*
>
> *But alas! How entirely unrelated to the world*
> *in which we live it has often been! How little has it*
> *had to offer to men and women who have never*
> *known our background and our kind of life, who*

are entirely ignorant of our very idiom and even our presuppositions. But in any case how detached and self-contained, how removed from a world that is seething in trouble with the foundations of everything that has been most highly prized rocking and shaking (The Plight of Man and the Power of God, p. 11).

What possibilities lie before Christians if only they are worthy of them! How little the world realizes the treasure that lies in its midst in the church of Jesus Christ. But how little the church realizes it, too. Think of what 300 million "qualified ministers of the new covenant" could accomplish around the world if they began to function as Paul lived. Will you bow your knees before the Father of our Lord Jesus Christ, and in his Name, cry: "Father, make me a qualified minister of the new covenant. Open my eyes to the full meaning of the truth that Jesus lives in me, by the Spirit. Make me to hunger and thirst after his righteousness, that according to your promise I might be filled. Amen."